AMERICA'S
CITY HALLS

William L. Lebovich
Historic American Buildings Survey

THE PRESERVATION PRESS

The Preservation Press
National Trust for Historic Preservation
1785 Massachusetts Avenue, N.W.
Washington, D.C. 20036

The National Trust for Historic Preservation in the United States is the only private, nonprofit national organization chartered by Congress to encourage public participation in the preservation of sites, buildings and objects significant in American history and culture. Support is provided by membership dues, endowment funds, contributions and grants from federal agencies, including the U.S. Department of the Interior, under provisions of the National Historic Preservation Act of 1966. For information about membership, write to the Trust at the above address.

Printed in the United States of America
88 87 86 85 84   5 4 3 2 1

Library of Congress Cataloging in Publication Data

America's city halls.
  Bibliography: p.
  Includes indexes.
  1. City halls—United States.   2. Historic buildings—
United States.   I. Historic American Buildings Survey.
NA4431.A47 1984   725'.13'0973   83-21310
ISBN 0-89133-115-8

This book is the accompanying publication to an exhibition prepared by the American Institute of Architects and the National Park Service and sponsored by the Smithsonian Institution Traveling Exhibition Service.

Designed by Marc Alain Meadows and Robert Wiser, Marc Meadows and Associates, Washington, D.C.
Composed in Bembo by Carver Photocomposition, Inc., Arlington, Va.
Printed on 80# Warren Patina by Collins Lithographing and Printing Company, Inc., Baltimore, Md.

Table of Contents

City Hall Features

Foreword

Every American city possesses a building that serves as the center of its government and community life. These city halls—because of their pivotal role in the lives of their cities—have become revered landmarks in many places. Their contributions to the development of their communities and American architecture cannot be overlooked. The examples in this book clearly show that the nation can be proud of its many municipal masterpieces. That so many remain to continue serving either as government offices or for wholly new uses is a tribute to their lasting quality and durability.

We feel sure that the cooperative project undertaken by the Historic American Buildings Survey of the National Park Service, the American Institute of Architects and the United States Conference of Mayors to document America's city halls will expand public knowledge and appreciation of these special community landmarks. This effort is aided considerably by the assistance of the National Trust for Historic Preservation in publishing this book and the Smithsonian Institution Traveling Exhibition Service in making available for communities across the country an exhibit on America's city halls prepared by the American Institute of Architects and the National Park Service.

Russell E. Dickenson
Director, National Park Service

George M. Notter, Jr., FAIA
President, American Institute of Architects

Richard H. Fulton
President, United States Conference of Mayors

Preface

The Historic American Buildings Survey project to record American city halls was undertaken to increase the documentation on this under-represented building type in the HABS collection at the Library of Congress. HABS, which marked its 50th anniversary in 1983, is the National Park Service's oldest historic preservation program and was founded for the purpose of documenting the architectural legacy of the nation for the education and benefit of the public. In doing so, the survey and its companion program, the Historic American Engineering Record, provide a source of information for historians of architecture and the general public. Since 1933 HABS has documented more than 16,000 significant examples of America's historic architecture. As a tribute to its half century of work, in 1983 the National Trust for Historic Preservation presented its highest honor, the Louise du Pont Crowninshield Award, to HABS.

To initiate the city halls project, a letter signed by the presidents of the American Institute of Architects and the United States Conference of Mayors and the secretary of the U.S. Department of the Interior was sent to the mayors and local AIA chapters of approximately 130 cities requesting their assistance in compiling histories and photographs of their communities' city halls. These 130 city halls were selected because they are either National Historic Landmarks or listed in the National Register of Historic Places or were cited as architecturally important by the staffs of the AIA, HABS or the Conference of Mayors. The project was not intended to be comprehensive in terms of the amount of documentation compiled or number of city halls documented.

The staff of the city government was responsible for writing the history, and the AIA chapter was responsible for providing photographs, both according to HABS guidelines. Histories and photographs were compiled on 119 city halls; of these, 114 have been included in the book. In most cases, both the city government and the local AIA chapter participated in the project, although in some instances the responsibility was handled entirely by one participant. In a few cases, the state historic preservation office provided the documentation. Occasionally, this information was supplemented by additional research of National Register forms, architectural guidebooks and history books.

The city halls are generally presented chronologically. At the end of each description are additional pertinent facts about the building: the dates of construction and the name of the architect, if known; the building's other names throughout its history; the building's current address, including county; and, if applicable, the designation of National Historic Landmark or National Register of Historic Places.

Fifty of the city halls documented for this project were included in an exhibition prepared by the AIA and HABS. The 50 represent the diversity of American city hall architecture from 1767 to the present. The exhibition, sponsored by the Smithsonian Institution Traveling Exhibition Service, is being shown in many of the cities included here. *America's City Halls* is the accompanying publication for the exhibition.

INTRODUCTION

CITY HALL

America's City Halls

The philosopher Friedrich Nietzsche (1844–1900) contended that "in architecture, the pride of man, his triumph over gravitation, his will to power, assume a visible form. Architecture is a sort of oratory of power by means of forms" *(The Twilight of the Idols)*. A city hall, then, can be seen as an oration of a local government's will to power, symbolizing triumph over the natural and human obstacles to its growth and prosperity. Taken collectively, America's city halls, therefore, symbolize the will to power of cities and towns as the United States became an ever increasingly urban country.

This examination of America's city halls begins with European antecedents and American colonial city halls and focuses on six major periods of American history: 1783–1861, 1865–92, 1893–1919, 1920–29, 1930–41, 1946–80. These dates, with the exception of the last one, were chosen because they coincide with events of national and international importance: the beginning and end of wars, depressions or other major occurrences. Although the correlation between national events, local events and city hall architecture is not precise, the relationships among these are compelling and justify using time blocks based not solely on municipal or architectural history but primarily on national history.

America's City Halls examines 114 existing city and town halls to discover the architectural characteristics of this building type and show how American city hall architecture evolved. Those forces that directly influenced the architecture of city halls and are reflected in that architecture are also considered here.

Boston's 17th-century town hall, drawn by Charles A. Lawrence, 1980, from the original specifications for Thomas Joy and Bartholomew Bernard, 1657. Courtesy of the Bostonian Society, Old State House.

European Antecedents and American Colonial City Halls

American city halls have their antecedents in 12th-century Europe, where the feudal order was collapsing and control of the towns was passing from the royalty and the church to urban inhabitants. To exercise these new responsibilities, citizens needed a place to assemble, discuss and promulgate rules; thus, the town hall emerged as a distinct building type. The early town hall was a two-story structure facing a plaza. The upper story housed one or more assembly halls and a few small rooms for records. The first floor housed an open, arcaded market; the vendors moved onto the plaza when additional space was needed. The hall's bell was rung to assemble the residents, and the bell tower became the symbol of the right of assembly—the keystone of town government. The oldest extant city hall is believed to be the Palazzo del Brotto (1215) in Como, Italy. It is a two-story polychromatic structure, with a round-arched arcade on the first floor and an adjacent bell and clock tower. Between 1250 and 1300, European town halls began to undergo a major organizational change. The first floor was enclosed for administrative use, and the market was moved to a separate building, not necessarily on the same plaza as the town hall. From 1300 to 1700, the European town hall did not become any further specialized, in terms of use, and it continued to house the council, the courts and administrative offices.

In the mid-17th century, colonial Boston built a town hall, unfortu-

14

nately no longer standing and not documented for this project, that, in terms of architecture and organization, was closely related to the medieval European town hall. Boston's half-timbered, relatively undecorated, two-story structure reflected the colony's limited craftsmanship and resources and its need for government offices. Atop the building were two open belfries, continuing the symbolism of the bell tower of the European town hall. To the side of the town hall were a stock and a whipping post for dispensing 17th-century justice. The elders who served as justices held court on the upper floor of the town hall, where space was also provided for public meetings and for an armory. The building's first floor was an open market. According to Bernard Bailyn, this building was the economic center of 17th-century Boston and New England and from it "radiated a large part of the commercial cords that laced New England to the other coastal ports, to the West, the Wind Islands, Spain, and especially to England" *(New England Merchants in the Seventeenth Century)*. The 17th-century British colonial town was primarily a mercantile endeavor, ruled by a merchant aristocracy, which promulgated laws predominantly concerned with regulating trade. The Boston town hall, paid for by the merchant Robert Keayne and housing both the market and the government, reflected these political realities.

The 17th-century American seaport functioned as the link between the wilderness and British markets. This role was explicitly encouraged by the British mercantile policy, which was intended to increase British economic and political control of the colonies. "This task of control could best be carried out if colonial life, and especially colonial economic life, was channeled through a limited number of focal points. At these points the imperial authorities could regulate trade and check illicit businesses," notes Charles Glaab (*A History of Urban America*). One result of this policy was to stimulate the growth of certain seaports; by 1730 Boston had 13,000 people, while New York had 8,000 and Philadelphia had 11,000.

Faced with burgeoning populations, the 18th-century colonial city governments passed fewer trade regulations than their 17th-century predecessors but passed more regulations concerned with the public welfare—sanitation, police, schooling and poverty. Despite this change in regulatory emphasis, the burden of providing these services still fell on private citizens. For example, the 18th-century city was protected by volunteer fire companies, a tradition that began in 1717 in Boston. There police patrols were also a private service, paid for by the city's wealthy. In the 18th century, as in the 17th, the executive, judicial and legislative responsibilities were all carried out by the assembly or council. The continuing importance of the city as a part of the trading network and the simple, undifferentiated nature of its government is suggested by Annapolis's city hall (1767–68). Designed by a carpenter, it consisted of only two rooms, an assembly room–ballroom and "His Lordship's Receiver General's Office," for collecting trading duties.

Throughout the colonial period, America's towns and cities were simple, smooth-running societies, with simple, dignified architecture and simple, limited governments. The urban historian Sam Bass Warner's description of colonial Philadelphia and its government is also applicable to the other colonial communities: "The wealthy presided over a

Annapolis City Hall

municipal regime of little government. . . . The municipal corporation of Philadelphia, copied from the forms of an old English borough, counted for little. Its only important functions in the late eighteenth century were the management of the markets and the holding of the Recorder's Court. A closed corporation, choosing its members by co-option, it had become a club of wealthy merchants, without much purse, power, or popularity. By modern standards the town was hardly governed at all" (*The Private City: Philadelphia in Three Periods of Its Growth*).

Early Republic, Urban Confusion, 1783–1861

Thomas Jefferson would have preferred that the young Republic have no cities: "I view great cities as pestilential to the morals, the health and the liberty of man" (quoted in *A History of Urban America*). Despite his sentiments, the size and number of American cities grew tremendously after the Revolution. From the first diennial census of 1790 to 1860, this country's urban population increased 30-fold, from 201,655 people (5 percent of the nation's population) to 6,216,518 (20 percent). By 1800 the United States had only two cities with more than 50,000 people—New York and Philadelphia; by 1850 they each had more than 100,000 inhabitants and were among the world's largest cities. Baltimore, Boston, New Orleans and Cincinnati also each had at least 100,000 citizens by mid-century, while St. Louis, Pittsburgh, Albany and Troy each had 50,000, and Providence, Washington, D.C., Charleston, Louisville and Buffalo were at the 10,000 mark. The growth of both the earlier, established coastal cities and the more recently founded inland towns and outposts was due to immigration, increased international trading opportunities, the introduction of American manufacturing and improved means for moving trade goods within the country—first the national roads, then the canals in the 1820s and finally the railroad from the 1830s.

New York City Hall

However, the tremendous growth of cities during the pre–Civil War period created unsafe, unhealthy urban environments that could not be controlled by the existing combination of limited municipal activity and privately funded agencies. The municipal governments attempted to address the problems by assuming greater responsibility and control for municipal services without improving the organization of the government. And at the same time, the local governments' prestige and powers were being eroded by the state legislatures. The resulting municipal government system was inadequate and led directly to the corruption of the post–Civil War period and reform movements of the late 19th and early 20th centuries. According to Charles Glaab, "In part, the problems of city government were simply the result of growth. Governmental structures that had been adequate for cities of 25,000 or fewer inhabitants were strained beyond their capacities as the great nineteenth-century urban agglomerations grew. But despite the obvious need there was no real effort to rebuild city government until the end of the century" (*A History of Urban America*).

From the founding of the Republic until the early 1820s, most cities continued with the same form of municipal government they had had as British colonies. Boston, for example, did not institute a mayoral system until 1822; before then, it held town meetings, and administration of the

Wilmington, Del., Old Town Hall

government was overseen by the Board of Selectmen. These selectmen were still drawn from the moneyed aristocracy because they were not remunerated, and they were not expected to devote their full time to their civic duties. Charles Bulfinch, for example, served as chairman of the Board of Selectmen and superintendent of police for 18 years, from 1799 to 1817, while practicing architecture.

Bulfinch did not get to design a city hall for Boston, but if he had it probably would have been in the Federal style, influenced by the highly colorful and decorative style of the British architects Robert, James and John Adam. Such a Federal-style city hall was built for Wilmington, Del., between 1798 and 1800. At that time, the building technology and architectural styles were sufficiently simple that the city councilmen designed the building without the assistance of an architect. As with other Federal-style buildings, the two-story Wilmington City Hall depended on delicate, occasionally elaborate detailing to provide interest. The belfry is characteristic of the early European and American city halls. The administrative needs of the Wilmington government were sufficiently simple that the building's entire first floor was designed and used as an assembly hall–ballroom, with only limited office space provided on the second floor. Even in a much larger municipality such as New York, the city administration was quite limited and therefore required little office space; in 1810 New York's population was 100,000, yet the city budget was only $100,000. New York City Hall (1803–11), designed as a French Renaissance interpretation of classical architecture, with Federal-style decorations, consists primarily of grand public and ceremonial spaces, such as the first-floor stair rotunda and second-floor hearing and reception rooms. New York City Hall was designed by the French-born architect Joseph Mangin and the American architect John McComb, who had been apprenticed to his builder-father.

Events of the 1820s and 1830s further decreased the city government's limited administrative role and power as the state's role increased. New York, for example, was but one of many cities that were issued new charters by the states in the early 19th century. A city's charter, under British colonial rule, had been considered inviolate, having been issued by the Crown. The new charter was perceived as more susceptible to modification and a reflection of state dominance over the city. Glaab observes, "Cities appeared to be losing powers steadily as the nineteenth century wore on. The revolution had, perhaps ironically, depressed the value of cities' 'charter rights'; when the State legislatures took over the power of granting city charters, the charters themselves became mere statutes alterable at will or even repealable by the bodies that passed them. These documents lost whatever 'prescriptive' or contractual status they had in the Colonial period, and the incorporated cities and towns became simply legal creatures of the State government" (*A History of Urban America*).

Indicative of the state's importance in municipal affairs were the circumstances surrounding the building of Salem (Mass.) City Hall (1837–38), funded by monies distributed by the commonwealth of Massachusetts. This building was designed in the classical revival style, which was substantially influenced by classical ruins and promulgated by Americans, such as Thomas Jefferson, who had visited France and had

Salem City Hall

studied the designs of contemporary French architects. Jefferson, who was U.S. Minister to France from 1784 and 1789, was an early advocate of an American architecture that symbolically expressed independence from England and suggested a philosophical similarity between this young democracy and those of ancient Rome and Greece. The classical revival style, also called the Greek Revival, was popular for residences and institutional buildings, as well as city halls, and was the predominant American architectural style between 1820 and 1860.

During this period, the absence of public services and the inadequacies of privately provided ones led to increasingly unattractive, unhealthy and unsafe cities. Many cities depended on farmers to run their hogs through the streets to scavenge the refuse. An 1844 *New World* editorial stated that New York's streets were "more abominably filthy than ever; they are too foul to serve as the styes for the hogs which perambulate them. . . . The offal and filth, of which there are loads thrown from the houses in defiance of an ordinance which is never enforced, is scraped up with the usual deposits of mud and manure into big heaps and left for weeks together on the side of the street." The sewage also contaminated the inadequate private water system, resulting in unsafe drinking water. Such unsanitary conditions helped spread diseases such as dysentery and typhus. In New Orleans in 1852, 8,000 people died of yellow fever, the third major outbreak in the United States since 1793, when Philadelphia lost 4,000 people, or 10 percent of its population, to the disease. Cholera epidemics occurred in 1832, 1849 and 1866.

The untrained, nonuniformed night watchmen and day patrolmen, mostly privately funded, were unable to prevent the rise of urban gangs and riots. According to Glaab, colonial American cities had been spared the "criminal districts and criminal gangs characteristic of European cities. By the 1840s, however, leaders in New York and elsewhere were concerned about the appearance of both phenomena" (*A History of Urban America*). Even as early as 1825, rioting became so uncontrollable in Boston that mayor Josiah Quincy had to lead a posse to restore order. The fire-fighting system, which depended on private companies, with some public funding, was no better than the police. Structures whose owners had not subscribed to a private fire-fighting company might be allowed to burn; on occasion, drunken rival companies were more occupied with brawling with each other than saving buildings. The hazards of urban living that Jefferson had been so aware of in the late 18th century continued to worsen in the 19th century.

Cities responded at different rates and in varying degrees to these inhumane conditions. Although the first municipal water system was designed by Benjamin Latrobe for Philadelphia in 1801, New York and Boston did not start building such systems until 1846 and Chicago and Baltimore not until a decade later. Despite the fact that several cities had created public health boards early in the century—New York in 1805, Philadelphia in 1818 and Chicago in 1837—it was not until 1866 that any city provided a staff for the board of health. As with public health services, municipal street cleaning did not begin until after the Civil War. However, sewage disposal was undertaken earlier; Boston assumed responsibility for this service in 1849 and Chicago in 1856. Cincinnati created the first paid municipal fire department in 1853. In the same year

Brooklyn Borough Hall

Gallier Hall

Wilmington, N.C., City Hall/
Thalian Hall

Mobile City Hall

New York created its board of police commissioners, providing effective management of the police department, which had been established in 1844. Philadelphia established its department in 1850, Boston in 1854 and Baltimore in 1857. The cities' switch from private patrols to privately and publicly funded patrols to uniformed, professional police forces had taken several years. By the time of the Civil War, the responsibility for providing municipal services, to the degree that they were available, had shifted from the private sector to the public, and the actual providers of these services were becoming professionals, receiving at least some training and getting paid.

At the same time that the cities were forming professional fire and police departments, architects organized in recognition of their emergence as professionals. In 1857 in New York, 12 architects founded the American Institute of Architects "to unite in fellowship the architects of this continent and to combine their efforts to promote the artistic, esthetic, scientific and practical efficiency of the profession." Beneath their lofty goals was the knowledge that anyone, at this time, could list himself as an architect and design buildings. For example, Gamaliel King, the designer of Brooklyn Borough Hall (1845–49), formerly Brooklyn's city hall, listed himself as an architect in the city directory when he designed this classical revival building, but previously he was listed as a builder and even earlier as a grocer. The best-educated or trained designers were the foreign-born architects and American gentlemen architects. For example, New Orleans's classical revival–style city hall (1845–50) was designed by the Irish-born architect James Gallier, who was one of this country's most skilled designers in that particular style.

In the same decade that firefighters, policemen and architects became professionalized, Wilmington, N.C., and Mobile, Ala., built Italianate-style city halls. Stylistically, these city halls represented the current taste in architecture, as the popularity of the classical revival style was waning and professional architects were working in a variety of styles. Under the influence of the architect A. J. Davis and the landscape architect A. J. Downing, architects often tried to fit the building's style to its purpose. Some prisons and cemetery structures, for example, were done in the oppressive and other-worldly Egyptian Revival style. The Gothic style seemed especially appropriate for churches. Although the city halls of Wilmington (1855–58) and Mobile (1855–57) were architecturally fashionable, functionally they hark back to the city halls that had been erected in the 17th and 18th centuries. Like Boston's town hall of 1657, Mobile's combines a city hall with a market and an armory. Wilmington's suggests comparison with the 1798 Wilmington, Del., city hall; both buildings' primary space was an assembly hall, with the secondary space for administrative use. Neither Wilmington, Mobile nor any other city hall built in the antebellum period reflected the increased responsibilities assumed by municipal government; only if the increased responsibilities had led to changes in the organization of city government would they have affected the architecture of city halls. At the risk of extending a metaphor too far, Wilmington City Hall, with its Italianate body and classical revival portico, symbolizes the dichotomous state of antebellum municipal government: increased responsibilities with decreased power.

Gilded Age Cities, 1865–92

Mark Twain and Charles Warner's 1873 satire on American greed, corruption and speculative fever indelibly labeled the post–Civil War period as the Gilded Age. Even a hundred years later, historians reiterate Twain and Warner's indictment: "In the growing industrial centers the war begotten wealth made Americans a vulgar, gluttonous, avaricious people. Misbehavior and corruption were by no means confined to public life, but they were more noticeable there . . ." (*American History at a Glance*). The symbols of misbehavior and corruption were the urban political bosses—portrayed by contemporary cartoonists as corpulent, cigar-smoking, derbied men, their pockets bulging with ill-gotten dollars—who ruled the cities as they grew from a collective population of 9,902,361 (25.7 percent of the national population) in 1870 to 22,106,265 (35 percent) in 1890. In reality, however, the bosses were also responsible for effectively providing new and expanded services, and the post–Civil War cities were not without their considerable accomplishments. There was rapid growth in technology and transportation systems, and during this period some of this country's most impressive city halls were built.

The most spectacular of these is Philadelphia City Hall (1871–1901). Its story is in microcosm the history of postbellum American cities. Philadelphia had needed a new city hall since 1854, when it annexed neighboring towns, forming a city with more than 500,000 people, double its previous size, and whose boundaries were now coterminus with those of the county. Such forced consolidation between a city and its smaller neighbors and the erection of a joint city hall–county courthouse (even where the boundaries of the city and county were not coterminus) were common throughout the second half of the 19th century and somewhat less common in the 20th century. In 1854 Philadelphia was still occupying its Federal-style, two-story city hall, built in 1790 adjacent to Independence Hall, but it was no longer adequate for the needs of the government of the expanded city. A state commission was appointed to erect the building, a reflection of the state's control of the city's financial affairs in the 19th century, and a competition was held for the design of the city hall. The project was delayed by the Civil War, after which a second competition, also won by John McArthur, was held. When the cornerstone ceremonies were finally held in 1874, one speaker said of the as yet uncompleted building: ". . . the whole effect is one of massive dignity worthy of us and our posterity. . . . From the north side rises a grand tower which will gracefully adorn the public buildings, and at the same time will be a crowning feature of the city, as St. Peter's is of Rome, and St. Paul's of London . . ." ("Philadelphia City Hall: Monster or Masterpiece?"). Philadelphia, having already surpassed all other American cities, saw itself as the equal of the European capitals.

Philadelphia's pretensions and rivalries are embodied in its city hall building. Its architectural style—the Second Empire style, made popular by the building of the new Louvre in Paris (1854–80)—put the building on a par with those of Paris. This style was chosen also by several other American cities for their municipal buildings, but Philadelphia City Hall outshone them all. The Second Empire style, best known for its mansard roofs, was intricate, intense and three-dimensional architecture, well

Philadelphia City Hall

Boston Old City Hall

Baltimore City Hall

Alexandria City Hall

expressed by Philadelphia City Hall, with its exquisite Alexander Calder sculpture, massive tower and pavilions, multistory and elaborately decorated interiors and the integration of the separate parts of the building. Boston's Old City Hall (1862–65), the earliest and one of the smallest Second Empire–style city halls, only hints at the movement, massing and detailing so powerfully expressed in Philadelphia's city hall. Between these two extremes lie Providence's city hall (1874–78), which is fairly close in size and modesty to Boston's, and those of Baltimore (1867–75), Norwich (1870–73), Louisville (1870–73) and Alexandria (1871–73), which are closer in size to Philadelphia's. The style was equally popular for residences, offices, institutional buildings and federal government buildings such as the magnificent State, War and Navy Building (1871–88) in Washington, D.C., and the St. Louis Post Office and Customhouse (1873–84), both by Alfred B. Mullett, supervising architect of the Treasury Department.

Because Philadelphia City Hall cost the then-staggering and still considerable amount of $20 million, it is not surprising that it is a tour de force. However, the building's huge cost was due not only to its architectural quality but also to municipal corruption. The Philadelphia historian John Maass wrote of the project: "No scheme begun in corruption, pursued in corruption and reeking with rottenness from skin to core, can be consummated in any other way than by open and unblushing crime" ("Philadelphia City Hall: Monster or Masterpiece?").

Huge municipal projects such as this enabled the bosses to reward their cronies and strengthen their hold on municipal affairs, as the urban historian Howard Gillette points out in his discussion of the Philadelphia City Hall project: "The erection of City Hall, originally directed and conceived as a public service, opened the way to political patronage and favoritism on a new scale. From there, however, Philadelphia politicians conceived an alliance which merged the traditional patronage of public works with public services, particularly street railways . . ." ("Philadelphia's City Hall: Monument to a New Political Machine"). In fact, the streetcar railways' main exchange was at the city hall, reinforcing the importance of the building and continuing the historical importance of its site, which had been a major intersection in the center of William Penn's original 17th-century plot for Philadelphia. The tradition of building city halls at prominent central locations, often on land reserved for that purpose, in this country dates at least to the 17th century with the Boston town hall, which also provided space for assembly halls and a market, and has continued into the 20th century. That second tradition of combining assembly halls and market in the city hall continued into the late 19th century, with Alexandria City Hall (1871–73) a Second Empire–style example.

The introduction of the streetcar railway at midcentury permanently changed the appearance of the American city. The compact American city of the colonial and antebellum periods, in which everything and everyone was within walking distance, was replaced by the extended city, where the distant suburbs were linked, first by horse-drawn and later by motorized streetcar railways. At the same time that the streetcar encouraged the development of low-density suburbs as residential areas for the city, the invention of the safe passenger elevator in 1857 encouraged the development of high-density central-city districts for commercial areas. Before the introduction of the elevator, buildings were usually limited to the five- or six-story heights people were accustomed to and willing to climb. With the elevator in place, the building height was determined not by the capacity of human locomotion but by the limits of building technology and economic feasibility. And Philadelphia City Hall, which was designed for elevators, pushed existing building technology to its limits; the building was the world's tallest structure with masonry-bearing walls. Advances in technology facilitated communications within cities, between cities and between countries. The telegraph was invented in 1837, and the trans-Atlantic cable was completed in 1866. The typewriter was invented in 1867, the telephone in 1876 and the tintype in 1886.

Spurred by annexations, technological changes, immigration (from rural areas and from Europe) and population increases, the postbellum American city grew rapidly and demanded greater services from its municipal government. Still hampered by state interference and lacking a strong administrative mechanism, postbellum municipal government was even more inadequate than its antebellum predecessor. In stepped the boss and his machine to provide the necessary services. The boss often occupied minor city, county, state or even federal elective office but usually did not serve as mayor. He controlled city government by dispensing patronage jobs and contracts. Reform-minded Theodore Roosevelt explained in 1866 the success and staying power of the boss in terms of the services he provided the less affluent, less powerful city inhabitant: "Voters of the laboring class are very emotional . . . if a man is open handed and warmhearted, they consider it as being a fair offset to his being a little shaky when it comes to applying the eighth commandment to affairs of state" (quoted in *A History of Urban America*). From a less individualistic, more institutional perspective, Charles Glaab has argued that the boss and his machine were critical to the functioning of the city: "In the complicated and badly designed formal structures of the city governments, with mayors and councils (sometimes bicameral) supposed to check and balance each other, with independent and partly independent commissions existing beside them, and with lines of legal authority and responsibility hopelessly confused, there was not only opportunity but also need for effective control—which almost had to be informal. This control was provided by the bosses and their machines. At whatever the price, streets did get paved, lighting, heat, telephone and transportation services were provided, and fire and police forces grew" (*A History of Urban America*).

As Glaab implies, the cost of corrupt municipal government was considerable. The Tammany Hall machine defrauded New York of at least $75 million. The utility companies bribed city officials to ensure favorable agreements, resulting in lost tax and leasing revenues to the cities. Detroit's mayor, Hazen Pingree, wrote in the 1890s that the utility companies "are responsible for nearly all the thieving and boodling with which cities are made to suffer from their servants. They seek almost uniformly to secure what they want by means of bribes, and in this way they corrupt our councils and commissions" (quoted in *A History of Urban America*). Graft drove up the cost of municipal buildings, as with

Richmond City Hall

Albany City Hall

J. THOMAS COCHRAN
Executive Director

Charleston, S.C.
June 18, 1989

Dear Mayor,

At our 57th Annual Conference we will feature our city halls. On display in our plenary hall you will see the Smithsonian Travelling Exhibition entitled "America's City Halls". This project is a cooperative effort by the Historical Buildings Survey of the National Park Service, American Institute of Architects - and - of course - THE UNITED STATES CONFERENCE OF MAYORS!

I'm pleased to present you this copy. Published by the National Trust for Historic Preservation, this book gives you a replica of the exhibit to take home from Charleston. Please read the introduction pages 14-36 for an interesting and concise history of the urban movement in our country.

The foreword reads "Every American city possesses a building that serves as the center of its government and community life" Inside these buildings are men and women from all walks of life - who - once elected - become the catalysts for energy within our cities. As you daily do your best to make it better for the people in your city who have honored you to work in your city hall, let us continue to work through the United States Conference of Mayors - sharing and supporting each other to make cities strong and compassionate for people living in cities.

Tom Cochran

Springfield, Ohio, Old City Hall

Brockton City Hall

Philadelphia City Hall. Another city hall marked by accusations of bribery and graft is Richmond City Hall (1886–94), a High Victorian Gothic building. Its architect, Elijah Myers, was accused of bribing the competition judges and giving kickbacks that caused time and cost overruns.

Often as architecturally powerful as Richmond City Hall are those buildings designed in the Richardsonian Romanesque style. The popularity of this style is suggested by the large number of Richardsonian Romanesque city halls documented here. The style is characterized by the use of massive, rough-faced stones on the exterior, the solidity of the arches and, most important, the integration of and balance between horizontal and vertical massing. H. H. Richardson contrasted the roughness of his exteriors by using light-colored woods and smooth-carved and polished stones on the interiors. Unfortunately, in the one city hall designed by him, for Albany (1881–83), he did not design the interiors. The most striking element of Albany City Hall is its bell tower, a motif dating to medieval city halls and one that Richardson's followers used, along with the characteristic rough-textured facing and interior-exterior contrast, in city halls such as those in Lowell (1890–93), Bay City (1894–97), Cambridge (1889), Minneapolis (built as a city-county building, 1889–1905) and Rochester (built as the U.S. Post Office and Courthouse, 1884–91). The least typical of the Richardsonian Romanesque city halls, in terms of massing and detailing, is the one in Springfield, Ohio (1888–90), which housed a gymnasium, farmers market and opera houses, in addition to administrative offices. By the time Brockton City Hall (1892–94) was built, the Richardsonian Romanesque had lost considerable popularity—Richardson had died in 1886 at the age of 48—and the change in taste is reflected in this building. Although a Richardsonian tower and openings are present, the surfaces are smooth and small scaled, and surface ornamentation suggests the influence of Louis Sullivan, who succeeded Richardson as one of America's foremost architects.

The construction of Brockton City Hall coincided not only with the end of the Richardsonian Romanesque but also with the end of the Gilded Age, a period of tremendous contradictions. At the national and municipal levels, the formal government structure lacked direction, yet it was a time of great growth in government. The historians Marshall Smelser and Joan Gunderson note, "Certainly the national administrations rarely led any of those significant movements" (*American History at a Glance*). Yet the United States expanded to include Alaska and the western plains and made inroads in controlling Hawaii. At the local level, undirected city governments substantially increased their geographic area and services. In both cases, growth was due, at least in part, to the informal coalition of business leaders and political bosses such as, at the national level, Mark Hanna, confidante of President William McKinley, and, at the local level, New York political boss William M. Tweed. In this period known for personal and political corruption at both the national and local levels, efforts at reform and public philanthropy also were made. The corruption of the local political machine has been discussed; one example of corruption at the national political level was the indictment in 1875 of 238 people, including President U.S. Grant's private secretary, for defrauding the federal govenment. By contrast, in 1883 Congress passed the Pendleton Act to reform federal patronage policies. Boss Tweed supported reform charters for New York in 1867 and 1870. During the period, Andrew Carnegie formulated his philosophy of philanthropy that resulted in his giving away most of his profits from the sale of Carnegie Steel. At the local level, philanthropists donated city hall buildings or, in the case of Cambridge, Mass., donated the land. At the same time that city hall buildings were a source of graft and architects were accused of winning these commissions through deals, more cities were using architectural competitions, which were supposed to make the process of selecting city hall architects impartial. Mark Twain and Charles Warner's *Gilded Age* is best remembered for its pessimistic view of America after the Civil War, but the authors also noted the country's naive optimism; at all levels and in all endeavors, government during the Gilded Age displayed the best and worst of motivations.

The Age of Discipline and Imperialism, 1893–1919

The years 1893 and 1894 were symbolic watersheds in American urban history. Events in those years offered alternatives to the architectural and governmental chaos of the late 19th-century city. The World's Columbian Exposition, held in 1893 in Chicago, provided a planned, disciplined vision of what the American city could look like. The next year, the National Municipal League was formed in Philadelphia and declared its intent to reform municipal government, "the one conspicuous failure of American democracy," according to Lord Bryce, late 19th-century British ambassador to the United States. However, it was not until 1900, when the urban population was 30,214,832 (39.6 percent of the country's population), that any significant institutional reform occurred in city government. And it was not until about 1910, when the urban population was 42,064,001 (45.6 percent) that the lessons of the exposition were applied and long-lasting government reform began. The end of World War I, in 1919, marked the close of this period of disciplined reform in the fields of architecture, urban planning and municipal government.

The 1893 exposition, commemorating the 400th anniversary of the discovery of America, was immensely popular. When President Grover Cleveland opened the fair on May 1, 1893, more than half a million people attended the ceremonies. In the mere six months that the exposition was open, there were 27,529,400 admissions, yet the population of the country was only slightly more than 70 million.

The fair's popularity was not limited to the masses. The historian and social critic Henry Adams devoted a chapter in his autobiography to the exposition. Novelist William Dean Howells saw in the planning of the exposition the beginning of a "socialistic state where destructive capitalism would be supplanted by a planned state working for the common good" (quoted in *Burnham of Chicago: Architect and Planner*). Harvard's preeminent art historian, Charles Eliot Norton, said that the exposition's Court of Honor made "a splendid display of monumental architecture. They show well how our ablest architects have studied the work of the past; and the arrangement of buildings according to the general plan produces a superb effect in the successful grouping in harmonious rela-

Court of Honor, World's Columbian
Exposition (view from east to west).
Courtesy of Chicago Historical Society.

tionships of vast and magnificent structures" (quoted in *Burnham of Chicago: Architect and Planner*).

The Court of Honor, the major axis of the exposition, was a long lagoon flanked by the fair's major buildings, designed by the country's most important architects. This axis had two foci: At the eastern end was the Administration Building, designed by Richard Morris Hunt, considered the dean of American architects; at the opposite end of the lagoon was the sculpture *The Republic,* by Daniel Chester French. Short cross-axes ran off the major axis, providing access to the secondary exposition buildings by boats or sidewalks flanking the waterway axes. The formal plan of the exposition was devised by the landscape architect Frederick Law Olmsted and architect Daniel H. Burnham, the exposition's chief of construction. With its visual foci and major and minor cross-axes, the exposition reflected the type of planning emphasized at the Ecole des Beaux-Arts in Paris. And what Norton described as the fair's "monumental architecture" that showed "well how our ablest architects have studied the work of the past" was the style of classical architecture taught at the Ecole. With but three exceptions, the fair's buildings displayed the domes, arched openings and columns characteristic of the Beaux-Arts classical style. According to a contemporary account, "the buildings were painted by spraying machines and covered with a composition resembling marble, which gave the fair the name of the 'White City'" (*Messages and Papers of the Presidents*). Given the uniformity of color, cornice height and architectural vocabulary, it is easy to understand how the fair provided a harmonious, compelling image that, in the opinion of the journalist Henry Demarest Lloyd, "revealed to the people possibilities of social beauty, utility, and harmony of which they had not been able to even dream. No such vision could otherwise have entered into the drudgery of their lives, and it will be felt in their development into the third and fourth generation" (quoted in *Burnham of Chicago:*

Architect and Planner).

Not all critics were as sanguine as Lloyd concerning the influence of the exposition on architecture. Thirty years later the architect Louis Sullivan described the influence of the fair as that of a virus that had killed off what was original in American architecture. The insightful contemporary architecture critic Montgomery Schuyler wrote that "doubtless the influence of the most admired group of buildings ever erected in this country, the public buildings at Washington not excepted, must be great," but he feared that the fair would generate uninspired copying of classical architecture (*American Architecture and Other Writings*).

The immediate effect of the exposition was to further increase the influence of the Ecole des Beaux-Arts and reinforce the already existing interest in revival architecture. Schuyler attributed the choice of classical architecture for the exposition to the Ecole's influence. "It [the study of classical architecture] is an indispensable part wherever the training is administered academically, and most of all at Paris, of which the influence upon our own architecture is manifestly increasing and is at present dominant. Most of the architects of the World's Fair are of Parisian training, and those of them who are not have felt the influence of that contemporary school of architecture which is most highly organized and possesses the longest and most powerful tradition." In the 1890s, 152 Americans attended the Ecole, compared with 10 in the 1860s, 33 in the 1870s and 29 in the 1880s. In 1894, 72 American architects founded the Society of Beaux-Arts Architects to disseminate the philosophy of the Ecole. In that same year only 3 out of the 8 American architecture schools had Ecole-trained faculty, but by 1911 all 20 architecture schools did.

Reflecting the influence of the Ecole des Beaux-Arts was the chateauesque St. Louis City Hall (1890–1904), whose French style is especially appropriate for this river city founded by French explorers. St. Louis City Hall has the monumental public spaces (staircases, council chambers, halls), successful integration of parts to form a harmonious whole and extensive surface decoration that are characteristic of Beaux-Arts architecture. But it would still be 20 years after the beginning of construction of St. Louis City Hall before the Beaux-Arts urban planning concepts demonstrated at the exposition and its most important lesson—the importance of large-scale planning—would be applied in city and civic center plans.

Progress in municipal government reform also was slow. The platform of the National Municipal League, formed in Philadelphia in 1894, called for the reform of city government through the institution of the short ballot (reducing the number of elective offices and increasing the number of positions filled by mayoral appointment), strengthening the administrative and fiscal powers of the mayor, municipal ownership of utilities, free public services, professionalism of public employment and development of merit pay, municipal home rule, nonpartisanship and at-large election of council members, the use of the initiative and recall, and the application of city-planning principles. During the 19th century, these reforms were instituted to varying degrees, all with limited effect because they were directed at changing symptoms of the troubled system of municipal governance rather than the system itself. Beginning in the 1880s, the power of the mayor increased steadily at the expense of the

St. Louis City Hall

powers of the city council. Gilded Age reformers believed that a stronger mayor with veto power over the budget could curtail the patronage politics of the city council. The theory had two faults: It assumed that the mayor would be free of the political machine, and it assumed that reform mayors would serve forever. In reality, political machines have continued to exist well into the 20th century, and, even after being voted out in reform movements, the machines have resumed power after one or two terms of reform mayors. As the perceptive Lord Bryce observed, ". . . in great cities the forces that attack and prevent democratic government are exceptionally numerous, the defensive forces that protect it exceptionally ill placed for resistance. Satan has turned his heaviest batteries on the weakest part of the ramparts" (quoted in *A History of Urban America*). One of the earliest and most prominent reform mayors was Grover Cleveland, who spent one year (1891) vetoing pork-barrel budgets in Buffalo, was elected governor the next year and was elected president in 1894. Although Cleveland continued to be a reform politician, Buffalo directly benefited for only one year.

Only in the 20th century was the basic institution of municipal government reformed—by being replaced. In 1900 Galveston was struck by a hurricane and tidal wave that killed one-sixth of the population and destroyed one-third of the property. Because the existing city government was unable to manage the devastated city, the state legislature appointed five commissioners to direct the clean-up and recovery. Four of the commissioners each had direct responsibility for a municipal agency, while the fifth served as mayor-coordinator. This commission form of government worked so well that the Texas legislature continued it under Galveston's new charter of 1903; the system was instituted in other cities in other states. Des Moines voted for the commission system in 1909 to replace a corrupt city government and, in the same election, voted funds for a new building to house the new government. Its Beaux-Arts city hall (1910–11) was clearly intended as the architectural symbol of the new government. In the building's main room, the counting room, city workers conducted their business in the open, under watchful public scrutiny. In that building there would be no private offices behind whose closed doors politicians could make deals at the expense of and without the knowledge of the public. Underlying the change from corrupt machine politics to honest, commission government, the new building was called the municipal building rather than the city hall, the latter term being associated with the previous discredited type of government. Despite its initial popularity, the commission form of government was quickly supplanted by the city manager form, in which a professional manager directed the daily operations of municipal government and supervised agency heads. The city manager, in turn, received directions from the mayor and council. Promoters of this system emphasized its similarity to the way a big business was run. The mayor and council were the equivalent of business stockholders, while the manager was the same as the president of the company, and below each were the department heads. This analogy was compelling to many municipal reformers, many of whom were conservative business people who were concerned with the extravagant cost of municipal government under the political machine. An early version of the manager form, with a quasiprofessional

Des Moines City Hall

manager, was instituted in Staunton, Va., in 1908. Sumter, S.C., is credited with having the first actual manager system in 1912, and Dayton was the first large city to institute the system in 1914. In the same year, eight city managers met in the Richardsonian Romanesque city hall (1888–90) in Springfield, Ohio, and formed the City Managers Association, an organization of professional city managers. By 1914, 32 cities had managers, and by the time the United States entered World War I in 1917, 100 municipalities had managers. (By 1976, 2,456 cities and towns used the manager system.)

When Des Moines was building its city hall, it was intended to be not only a symbol of its new government but also an element in a grouping of buildings that would form an appropriately monumental approach to the state capitol and enhance the river frontage. This complex was never built. Cleveland, under the impetus of local business leaders, was much more successful in implementing its urban plan. With Lake Erie as the focus, the city hall (1912–14) and other city, county, federal and private buildings having compatible Beaux-Arts facades were built around three sides of a large green. A more modest civic center, with a joint city-county building (1914–17), post office, library and hotel, was built in Wilmington, Del., in response to the urgings of the Du Pont Company.

The incorporation of city halls into civic center plans or even larger city plans, starting early in the 1900s but showing results only around 1910, was the most important outgrowth of the Columbian Exposition. Under the rubric of the City Beautiful Movement, the architect Daniel H. Burnham and his associates began applying the Beaux-Arts planning concepts they had used at the exposition in redesigning American cities. In these planning exercises, the architects and government leaders displayed their belief in disciplined, rational planning to ameliorate city problems and foster cooperation between the public and private sectors (e.g., the Cleveland plan) and cooperation among the various levels of government (e.g., the Wilmington plan). Part of this rational approach was the objective selection of architects through competitions; the use of architectural competitions for city hall commissions reached its peak during this period.

The Beaux-Arts concern with placing early 20th-century city halls within a larger context gives these city halls a civic quality lacking in the Second Empire–style and Richardsonian Romanesque city halls. These earlier city halls are free-standing buildings that call attention to themselves, often through the presence of towers, and they seem incapable of harmoniously coexisting with other buildings, even those in the same style. For example, it does not seem coincidental that the Philadelphia (1871–1901) and Minneapolis (1889–1905) city halls occupy entire blocks; they need to exist in isolation. Even Boston's Old City Hall (1862–65), which is built in one of the oldest and most congested parts of the city, has streets and an alley on three sides; the fourth side is essentially open, facing a burial ground and church. By contrast, Beaux-Arts city halls, whether designed as part of civic complexes or as independent projects, seem to consciously suggest that they are part of a larger unit, an element in a streetscape or in a group of buildings. All three styles— Second Empire, Richardsonian Romanesque and Beaux-Arts—produced monumental and forceful works, but the Beaux-Arts style also

Cleveland City Hall

Wilmington, Del., Public Building

San Francisco City Hall

Oakland City Hall

embellished some of its civic complexes with a grandeur and civility not achieved in the individual city halls of earlier periods.

The grandeur and civility of the whole complex might have been reached at the expense of the individual buildings within the complex. Montgomery Schuyler's observation on the Court of Honor at the Columbian Exposition was equally applicable to the City Beautiful civic complexes built approximately 20 years later: "In the first place the success is first of all a success of unity, a triumph of *ensemble*. The whole is better than any of its parts and greater than all its parts, and its effect is one and indivisible" (*American Architecture and Other Writings*).

In only one case was the city hall better than the whole—San Francisco City Hall (1913–15), the grandest Beaux-Arts city hall and the focus of the grandest Beaux-Arts civic center. The city hall has everything one expects in the best of Beaux-Arts buildings: It is monumental in whole and part, on the exterior and interior; exquisite attention was paid to detailing and massing; and the building is viewed and approached through monumental spaces created by nearly monumental background buildings. San Francisco's city hall and civic center represent the peak of Beaux-Arts architecture and planning, not only in terms of design but also because the architects were chosen by competition, the complex served city and county governments, it openly borrowed from acknowledged architectural masterpieces, and its buildings are not multipurpose.

With the exception of San Francisco's rival across the bay, Oakland City Hall (1911–14), which housed administrative offices, an emergency hospital, police department, courts, prison and fire department with dormitory, the Beaux-Arts city hall had become quite specialized, housing only administrative offices, not libraries, auditoriums, markets or the various facilities housed in Oakland City Hall or earlier city halls. This specialization and building of separate facilities for other departments reflected the growth and professionalization of city government and the Beaux-Arts emphasis on planning and developing multigovernment complexes.

The San Francisco civic complex was completed during World War I, before the United States entered the war. When President Woodrow Wilson addressed Congress on April 2, 1917, requesting a declaration of war against Germany, he spoke about America assuming its rightful place as a world leader: "To such a task we dedicate our lives, our fortunes, everything that we are and everything that we have, with the pride of those who know that the day has come when America is privileged to spend her blood and happiness and the peace which she has treasured" (*Documents of American History*). The concept of the United States as a world power and as an imperial power had its origins in the expansive and prosperous post–Civil War period, 1865–92. During that time this new self image was demonstrated in the annexation of Alaska and the increasing control over Hawaii. The first indisputable demonstration of this country's sense of destiny to be an imperial power was the Spanish-American War of 1898, which resulted in American control of the Philippines, Puerto Rico and Cuba. In the same year, a major domestic annexation also occurred, with New York absorbing the surrounding boroughs to create a city of more than 4 million people (approximately 14 percent of the U.S. urban population). But what distinguishes the acquisitive drive of the Gilded Age (1865–92) from that of the Age of Discipline and Imperialism (1893–1919) is that in the latter period discipline and planning were applied to municipal and overseas affairs. Unfortunately for cities, the widespread desire for further disciplining and reforming municipal government was replaced, when the United States entered World War I, by increasing interest in U.S. international ambitions. It is appropriate that this age of imperial ambitions, domestic and international, was ushered in with a world's fair designed in an architectural style based on that of imperial Rome, that this style of architecture was the most popular style during the period and that the period closed with the United States achieving its ambitions to be a world power.

Decade of Frivolity and Conservative Reaction, 1920–29

In a May 1920 campaign speech, presidential candidate Warren G. Harding proclaimed that "America's present need is not heroics but healing; not nostrums but normalcy; not revolution but restoration." Harding was elected, and the country lived the decade according to his advice. Turning against the disciplined municipal reforms, planning and internationalism of the previous period, Americans pursued two contradictory paths during the false, short-lived prosperity of the 1920s. It was a time of unequaled frivolity and scandal as well as fundamentalist morality and prejudice. It also was the first time that most Americans lived in urban areas; the 1920 census listed 54,157,973 people (51 percent of the population) as city dwellers.

Denver City and County Building

The frivolity of the age has been conveyed in the writings of F. Scott Fitzgerald and others. The period even had its own music—jazz—that captured the undisciplined frenzy of the day. The country also experienced political scandals that exceeded anything previously known. The director of the Veterans Bureau, along with associates, was convicted of having taken $200 million from companies serving disabled veterans. The alien property custodian was convicted of defrauding the government by accepting a bribe to sell below value German property confiscated by the United States during World War I. The attorney general was forced to resign because of allegations that he had taken bribes from bootleggers and had also failed to properly prosecute the alien property custodian and Veterans Bureau director. The secretary of the Interior became the first cabinet member to go to jail for malfeasance in office. He had taken approximately $400,000 in bribes to allow two oil companies to drill government oil reserves at Teapot Dome, Wyo., and Elk Hills, Calif.

The obverse side of the decade's frivolity and corruption was a conservative, regressive attitude expressed in the isolationist, temperance and fundamentalist movements. The United States began to restrict European immigration for the first time, the white supremacist Ku Klux Klan became increasingly active, 1928 presidential candidate Al Smith was the subject of an anti-Catholic campaign, and two Italian-American anarchists, Nicola Sacco and Bartolomeo Vanzetti, were convicted of murder and sentenced to death after a controversial trial. Temperance became the rule of the land under a constitutional amendment. The Volstead Act, creating the mechanism for carrying out the prohibition against alcoholic

Atlanta City Hall

Los Angeles City Hall

beverages, was passed over President Wilson's veto in October 1919 and remained in effect, but not effectively enforced, until 1933. The state of Tennessee enacted a law requiring that only the biblical explanation, the fundamentalist explanation, of creation could be taught in the schools. In 1925 John Scopes was brought to trial ("The Monkey Trial")for violating that law; he was defended by Clarence Darrow and prosecuted by the populist William Jennings Bryan. In a triumph of fundamentalism, Scopes was convicted. The degree to which Americans in the 1920s feared any radicalism and fervently desired a return to the values of an earlier period was expressed not only by the executions of Sacco and Vanzetti but also by the 1920 raids, authorized by Attorney General A. Mitchell Palmer, in which more than 4,000 suspected Communists were arrested, many of them illegally. During the 1920s, according to John Krout and Arnold S. Rice, "fear pervaded the nation that radicalism might destroy American traditions. Even the moderate reforms of the recent progressive era came under suspicion. As a result, some who had been reformers in their younger years now gained prominence as defenders of the existing economic and social order" (*United States Since 1865*).

City hall architecture and the architectural establishment reflected the country's mood. All of the 1920s city halls documented were designed in revival styles but not in the disciplined Beaux-Arts classicism of the previous period. Instead, the city hall architects had the newfound freedom to be frivolous, to draw from a variety of historic architectural sources—the American Georgian, as seen in the Denver City and County Building (1929–32), the American Indian, as in Phoenix (1928–29), and the Gothic, as in Littleton, Colo. (1920). The city halls in Pasadena (1926–27) and Coral Gables (1927–28) used Spanish styles and tried to apply the Beaux-Arts concepts of civic planning, but in both cases the results were less disciplined than those of the Beaux-Arts period. Only two city halls, the setback skyscraper built in Atlanta (1928–30) and the skyscraper in Los Angeles (1926–28), suggested any awareness of the bolder directions being taken in architecture. But Atlanta City Hall was faced in Gothic detailing like Cass Gilbert's earlier Woolworth Building (1911–13) in New York, and the Los Angeles city hall dedication brochure specifically stated that the design drew on traditional American motifs and had nothing to do with contemporary European architecture; therefore, the Los Angeles city hall was in keeping with the country's chauvinistic, anti-immigrant sentiments.

Ultimately, it was not a city hall but a ceremony of the American Institute of Architects—the architectural establishment—that demonstrated that architects were also caught up in the frivolity of the decade. On the evening of May 11, 1923, Henry Bacon, architect of the Lincoln Memorial (1911–12), was awarded the AIA's Gold Medal. First, Bacon and his fellow architects dined under a marquee on the Mall in Washington, D.C., and then proceeded to the reflecting pool in front of the Lincoln Memorial. Bacon and guests, in colored robes, were transported by barge the length of the pool. Finally, in a solemn ceremony on the steps of the monument, President Warren G. Harding presented Bacon with the Gold Medal. City hall architecture reflected the undisciplined eclecticism of the period while the architects' professional organization turned frivolity into architectural pageantry.

The frivolity ended abruptly when the stock market crashed on Black Thursday, October 24, 1929, when more than 13 million shares were traded. By November 14, stocks with a total face value of $30 billion were worthless, causing the financial ruin, Krout and Rice note, of "hundreds of thousands of Americans [who], for the first time, were buying securities (stocks and bonds) on the stock exchange; and many were acquiring their shares on credit" (*United States Since 1865*).

The Depression and Greater Federal Role in Urban Affairs, 1930–41

Schenectady City Hall

The Depression, precipitated by the stock market crash, continued to deepen during the remainder of President Herbert Hoover's term. By 1932 approximately 85,000 businesses, representing a total worth of $4.5 billion, failed. By late 1931, 10 million persons were unemployed, and their ranks swelled by another 4 million in 1932. The national income declined from $81 billion in 1929 to $53 billion in 1931 to $41 billion in 1932. In the presidential election of 1932, New York Governor Franklin D. Roosevelt decisively defeated Hoover. Roosevelt initiated two "New Deals" between 1933 and 1939, both aimed at getting Americans re-employed and reforming the American financial system, whose instability had led to the Depression. The 1930 urban population was 69,160,599 (56.1 percent of the total population); in 1940 it was 74,705,338 (56.5 percent of the total population).

Four federal relief programs most directly affected the cities by providing money to local governments for work-relief projects. In the first year of Roosevelt's term, Congress established the Civil Works Administration (CWA) and the Federal Emergency Relief Administration (FERA), both directed by Harry Hopkins, a close friend of Roosevelt, and the Public Works Administration (PWA), directed by Secretary of the Interior Harold Ickes. The CWA employed approximately 4 million persons in 1933 to repair roads and improve parks. The next year its responsibilities were absorbed by FERA, which matched the monies spent by local and state governments for relief projects.

Buffalo City Hall

Between 1933 and 1939, the PWA, in cooperation with local governments, spent approximately $5 billion and employed more than 500,000 persons on nearly 35,000 projects to construct roads and structures such as hospitals, dams and bridges. The PWA's Housing Division, concerned with clearing slums and building low-cost housing, had limited success. Ickes wrote, "I was very disappointed with the progress that has been made. There isn't any doubt that something is wrong in the Housing Division, in fact, has been wrong for a long time. We are not getting results" (quoted in *A History of Urban America*). In 1935 the Works Progress Administration (later renamed Work Projects Administration) was created; directed by Harry L. Hopkins, it spent approximately $11 billion by 1943. It funded manual laborers for the construction of roads and other municipal building projects, and it also funded highly skilled people, through the Federal Actors Project, the Federal Theater Project and the Federal Writers Project. City halls were renovated, repaired and constructed with funding from these federal work-relief programs.

The city halls built during the Depression fall into two categories of what can be viewed as escapist architecture—buildings evoking either

Kansas City City Hall

St. Paul City Hall

this country's glorious early days or a science-fiction future. The earliest (1930–31) in Schenectady, N.Y., counters the emotional gloom of the Depression by recalling America's past, specifically the time when the colonies won independence from the British monarchy. Schenectady, on the basis of an architectural competition, awarded the commission for a late Georgian-Federal revival–style city hall to McKim, Mead and White. The other city halls of the period appear to have dismissed the past and present, suggesting an imaginary future. With their monumental relief sculpture and murals, brightly decorated interior surfaces imitating exotic materials and stripped surfaces, these city halls evoke a future where the mighty state will protect and succor the weak individual. The sheer height and large mass of city halls such as Buffalo's (1929–31), St. Paul's (1930–31) and Kansas City's (1936–37) can be interpreted as meaning that the power of the government is greater than that of the individual. The escapist, futuristic characteristics of city hall architecture in the 1930s was echoed in Buck Rogers movies and the U.S. world's fairs, especially Chicago's Century of Progress Exposition (1933) and the New York World's Fair (1939), where a vision of a high-technology future was on display.

Whether the efforts of the Roosevelt administration would have been sufficient to eventually provide full employment and full utilization of factories is unknown. World War II curtailed the domestic programs but at the same time created military and manufacturing jobs for millions. The war further shifted power and attention away from municipal affairs and municipal government to national affairs and national government.

Suburbanization and Downtown Renewal, 1946–80

Starting after World War II, Americans in large numbers began to abandon the cities in search of new, relatively inexpensive housing outside the cities. This exodus occurred so rapidly and was of such magnitude that the U.S. Census Bureau revised its definition of the term "urban area" in advance of the 1950 census taking. Previously an urban area was defined as an incorporated area with a population of 2,500 or more persons. For the 1950 census and subsequent ones, the bureau defined the urban population as "all persons residing in urbanized areas and outside those areas, in all places incorporated *or unincorporated* which had 2,500 inhabitants or more." The Census Bureau realized that political boundaries no longer reflected the large shift of population out of the established cities; not to count as urban population the people living in the unincorporated suburbs of these cities would have grossly distorted the country's demographics. This rapid suburbanization of the country was brought to public attention in 1961 with the publication of geographer Jean Gotman's *Megalopolis,* in which he contended that because of suburbanization discrete urban, suburban and rural areas no longer existed; areas such as that between Washington, D.C., and Boston had become a "continuous sytem of deeply interwoven urban and suburban areas." The urban population in 1940 was 74,705,338 (56.5 percent of the U.S. population); in 1980, by contrast, it had more than doubled, reaching 167,050,992 (73.7 percent).

The growth of the suburbs was spurred, in large part, by the federal government. In the 1950s the government encouraged the building of interstate highways linking urban areas. Federal subsidies, reaching as high as 90 percent of the cost of construction of such highways, continued well into the 1970s. At the same time, the federal government was providing housing subsidies for new construction in the suburbs as a means of stimulating the postwar economy. The net result of these federal policies was to encourage suburbanization: Housing was being built in the suburbs, and the high-speed highways (and availability of cars) facilitated commuting between suburban housing and urban jobs.

With suburbanization came a proliferation of local governments. By the 1960s the New York metropolitan area had 1,400 separate governments and Chicago also had more than 1,000. To counter the confusion and difficulties caused by excessive, specialized and overlapping local government units, some areas consolidated their governments. The Davidson County Public Building and Court House (1936–37), Nashville, Tenn., for example, has since 1962 housed Metro Government, formed by the merger of city and county governments.

At the same time that many urban dwellers were moving to new houses in the suburbs, the federal government continued to spend billions to demolish and replace substandard urban housing. Only 893,500 units of low-cost housing, 143,000 of which were for the elderly, were built between 1933 and 1970. The relative insignificance of the amount of public housing erected in this 37-year period can be seen by comparing the number of private residential units—1,396,000—built in 1951 alone. According to urban historians such as Dwight Hoover, public opposition to subsidized housing and a major change in the housing laws account for the small number of units built. While the 1937 Housing Act restricted federal monies to pay for clearing slums for housing, the 1949 and 1954 Housing Acts gave the city redevelopment agencies discretion as to what could be built on the cleared sites. Since the mid-1950s, slums and deteriorated downtowns have increasingly been cleared not for housing but for civic, business and multiple-use centers.

Boston's government center, with its new city hall (1963–69) as the focus, is one of the earliest and best known of the federally funded civic centers. The inclusion of federal, state and city governments in the center, the use of a national architectural competition to pick the city hall architect and the siting of the building according to a comprehensive master plan are all suggestive of the early 20th-century City Beautiful civic centers. Boston City Hall, with its distinctive inverted pyramid shape, has been hailed as the symbol of the new Boston.

Other cities have also built new, unusual city halls as part of civic-center projects to symbolize the local government's commitment to the renewal of run-down urban areas. The city halls in midwestern cities such as Springfield, Ohio (1977–79), and western cities such as Tempe, Ariz. (1969–71), are recent examples.

By contrast, Kettering, Ohio, built a new city hall (1968–69) not as part of an urban renewal project but as the first city hall for this newly formed city. Its dramatic pyramid shape, like that of the Boston and Tempe city halls, suggests that the city wanted more than a purely functional administrative building. Kettering is an example of the new cities that developed because of post–World War II suburbanization; it

Boston City Hall

Springfield, Ohio, City Hall

Tempe City Hall

Kettering City Hall

intended its city hall to be a symbol of the new city, to help distinguish it from neighboring older, better-known cities.

In the period 1945–80, city governments became more dependent on the federal government for funding. For example, in 1939 the government contributed $85,210,000 of the $2,810,108,000 (3 percent) of the revenues of cities with populations of 100,000 or more. In 1970 the federal share was $31,081,000,000 of the $91,964,000,000 (38 percent) of these cities' revenues—an increase of more than 126 percent. Charles Glaab has written that by 1979 many cities "were dependent on Federal aid for survival. In 1978, Buffalo, the extreme example, received over 69 percent of its budget from the Federal Government, in striking contrast to only 2.1 percent in 1967. Federal funds constituted from one-fourth to one-half of total budgets in numerous other cities" (*A History of Urban America*). During this period the distinctions between cities and units of governments also had become less clear because of the formation of megalopolises. The unusual designs of recent city halls suggest that city leaders view city hall building projects as a means of creating new symbols of their cities to compensate for the loss of a distinctive identity.

Two Centuries of City Halls

The late architectural historian Sir Nikolaus Pevsner once characterized 700 years of European municipal government architecture as the story of increased specialization. Increased specialization, increased emphasis on the exterior and increased symbolic value, along with the reduced importance of city government, characterize 200 years of American city hall architecture.

In the unspecialized 17th-century Boston town hall, all government and commercial functions took place in one building. The first floor was the market, and the second was the assembly rooms and administrative offices for the entire government. Justice—that is, corporal punishment—was even administered in front of the building. By the time of the Revolution, specialization had led to the removal of the markets to another building or site. By the time of the Civil War, the functions of municipal government had become even more specialized, resulting in separate chambers for courts, city councils and mayors (with council chambers being used also for public assembly), and the jail was in the basement. Further specialization in the late 19th and early 20th century meant that various branches of government, such as the police and fire departments and the courts (with jails) had their own buildings and were no longer housed in the city hall. Also, fewer and fewer city halls had the community's largest assembly hall. Increasingly, separate auditoriums were built, and the city hall served one less function. City halls erected after World War II are specialized to the degree that they have become office buildings for housing city government. In some instances—Wilmington, Del., and Fairfield, Calif., for example—council chambers are housed in separate buildings rather than with the administrative offices, suggesting that the city hall has become so specialized as an office building that it would be out of keeping to have an assembly chamber in the building.

The more officelike city halls have become, the less impressive are the

Fairfield City Hall

interiors. The grand rotundas, halls and staircases of 19th- and early 20th-century city halls such as those in New York, Pittsburgh and San Francisco are absent from more recent city halls. The two- and occasionally three-story council chambers of the 19th century, with elaborate surface decorations, have been replaced in the 1960s and 1970s city halls by smaller, much simpler, more functional council rooms. As the city hall has become more specialized, it is visited less frequently by the public; subsequently, the public spaces are less important and, therefore, have become less impressive. The post–World War II city hall is one building type that shows that changing functional needs (simpler and fewer public spaces) coincide with changing architectural tastes (less decoration).

Concomitant with less emphasis on the interiors of city halls is a greater emphasis on the exterior. Although such a change in a building is gradual and occurs over several years, one city hall, Albany's (1881–83), exemplifies the trend. The building's powerful exterior, designed by H. H. Richardson, was thrown off balance by an interior designed by another architect. The city went with a mild Georgian revival design that, satisfying no one, was eventually replaced by a somewhat better design. The Beaux-Arts city halls of the early 20th century further emphasized the exterior of the building at the expense of the interior. The exterior of a Beaux-Arts city hall would have been designed to harmonize with the exterior treatments of other buildings in the civic center complex, creating a whole of greater architectural merit than any of the parts. Even in Cleveland and San Francisco's Beaux-Arts city halls, in which the interiors are still distinguished, they are not as important as the exteriors. In later city halls the emphasis continued to shift from a balanced treatment of exterior and interior to an overwheming concern with the exterior. The city halls of Boston, Dallas, San Bernardino and Tempe are four recent examples in which the architectural statement is primarily expressed through the design of the exterior.

Dallas City Hall

Before the Revolution, management of cities and towns was a relatively simple task. American society was more homogenous, and little was expected of government. By the Civil War, a more heterogeneous, less harmonious society expected and required much more of its municipal government. And the government was seldom able to respond adequately to the changed society and the new needs of the citizens. Urban violence and government corruption, common to the 19th and 20th centuries, are but two symptoms of the limited control exercised by local government. This power was further diminished with the tremendous influx of federal funds in the 1930s. Municipal governments became increasingly dependent on the national government, and it, in turn, gained a greater role in running the cities by specifying how its monies would be spent. Since the Revolution and more particularly since the Civil War, outside factors beyond the control of city government—e.g., new technology, population shifts, changes in cities' economic base and federal funding—have increasingly influenced the economic, social and physical state of the city, while the city government is less able to be influential.

With the decline in power of municipal government has come a decline in the importance of the building that houses city leaders. Few, if any,

San Bernardino City Hall

36

Bay City City Hall

Providence City Hall

would claim that the current Boston City Hall is the center of the city or the region, which is how the historian Bernard Bailyn described the 17th-century Boston town hall. Present-day Boston, like any large city, has banking, medical, government and financial buildings that eclipse the city hall in power and importance as architectural statements of the city. Despite the great merits of city halls in cities such as New York, Los Angeles and San Francisco, it is unlikely that these are the first buildings that come to mind when those cities are mentioned.

Regardless of the general perception of the city hall's reduced importance, local government views it as having great symbolic value—witness the major, dramatic city halls and municipal government centers built in the 1960s and 1970s. For some cities, these buildings were intended to symbolize the rebirth of the downtown (e.g., Springfield and San Bernardino), the birth of a new city (Kettering) or a new image for a city (Dallas). City halls as far back as those of 13th-century Europe have had a symbolic aspect—the city hall belfry symbolized the citizens' right of free assembly—but the symbolic aspect has been increasingly emphasized.

It is this characteristic that explains why New York, which has had a population of more than 7 million people for more than 40 years, continues to use its 1811 city hall, which was built when the city had fewer than 125,000 people. And this phenomenon suggests that other older city halls will continue to be either renovated and reused by the city government, as in Baltimore, Bay City, Mich., and Providence, or recycled, as in Lincoln, Neb., Richmond, Va., or Binghamton, N.Y. When city halls are built, they are intended to symbolize certain facets of a city. But over time, these buildings acquire additional associations and symbolic values. Perhaps above all else these city halls symbolize continuity, a value especially appreciated in times of turbulent change, which has characterized the entire existence of American cities. Even when city governments have felt the need for new symbols—to express progress or commitment to the downtown—and built new city halls, the old buildings have often been saved because the citizens have appreciated the symbolic and aesthetic values of the old landmarks.

Decisions to build, demolish or preserve city halls are never made entirely on the basis of the symbolic value of the building. Finances, political egos, the architectural merit of the building in question and functional needs are all important considerations. But lest anyone forget the importance of the intangible and symbolic value of city halls, it is appropriate to recall the words of Edwin O'Connor, whose *The Last Hurrah* was a fictional account of machine politics inspired by the career of Boston Mayor James M. Curley: "City Hall was a lunatic pile of a building: a great, grim, resolutely ugly dust-catcher which had been designed eighty years before by the then mayor, one Clement 'Nutsy' McGrath . . . . It was from this man's unskilled and laboriously drawn plans that the present City Hall had arisen, and for generations it had been decried as the prime eyesore of the community. Despite this, the building had its defenders, and intermittent suggestions that it be razed had met with howls of protest from those who had worked long within and who, with a certain rude poetic vision, saw in this inefficient, tangled warren the perfect symbol for municipal administration."

THE CITY HALLS

CITY HALL

Annapolis Municipal Building
Annapolis, Maryland

Built on the site of a mid-18th-century market house and intended for use as the city meeting space and revenue office, the municipal building also served the state government while the Maryland State Capitol (1772) was being built. From November 26, 1783, to June 3, 1784, Annapolis was also the national capital, and it is generally believed that the December 20, 1783, dinner given by Congress in honor of George Washington was held in this building. The ballroom was used for meetings, lectures, dances, concerts, exhibitions and other public functions. In 1867 the one-story building was raised to two stories, the ballroom was moved to the second floor and the Italianate details—pilasters, pediment, cornice and lintels—were added. Fifteen years later, two end bays were modified for use by Independent Fire Company No. 2. In 1974 a rear addition was built, the interiors were altered and the facade was restored to its 1867 appearance. The council chamber, on the second floor, appears to have been decorated with detailing from the 18th-century ballroom. The adjacent, lower building is an original part of the municipal building, but its facade dates from a remodeling that took place around 1910.

1767–68; 1867
City Ballroom, Assembly Room
150 Duke of Gloucester Street (Anne Arundel County)
National Register of Historic Places

Lancaster Old City Hall

Lancaster, Pennsylvania

Built as county offices, Lancaster's Old City Hall was designed and constructed by local craftsmen with advice from some of Philadelphia's master carpenters. The structure's small scale and flat, red-brick surfaces relieved by the white-frame, Adamesque doorway and white stone lintels are characteristic of Federal-style buildings erected during the late 18th and early 19th centuries. The building is located in the center of the city and is one of its oldest structures; it served as the state capitol from 1799 until 1812, when it was used as the county courthouse. From 1854 to 1931, the building was Lancaster's city hall; during that period, it also housed the town's first telephone facility, a school room and a short-lived museum. Alterations to the original structure include the addition of a third floor sometime before 1854 and changes in floor plan and appearance, including the addition of a pedimented doorway, resulting from its restoration in 1924 by Melvern R. Evans. Since 1973 the building has served as a museum for 18th- and 19th-century local art.

1795–98. John Lind, Jacob Weidman, Casper Brunner and Jacob Flubacher
Heritage Center, Public Offices
Penn Square (Lancaster County)
National Register of Historic Places

The Cabildo

New Orleans, Louisiana

Designed in a Spanish neoclassical style, the Cabildo was the site of the November 30, 1803, ceremony in which Spain retroceded Louisiana to France. Twenty days later, as provided by the terms of the Louisiana Purchase, the United States acquired the land from France. Built on the site of two government buildings destroyed in the fire of 1788, the building faces Jackson Square (formerly Place d'Armes) and is adjacent to St. Louis Cathedral. On the other side of the cathedral is the Presbytère. All three buildings were designed by Gilberto Guillemard, a Frenchman, and are in the neoclassical style, thus creating a satisfying symmetry. This style, marked by rounded openings flanked by simple, engaged columns and pilasters, was the preferred style for Spanish colonial government buildings. The Cabildo served as New Orleans's city hall from 1803 to 1836, when the state revoked the city's charter and divided it into three municipalities under one mayor. Until the reunification of the city in 1852, the Cabildo served as the municipal hall for the Creole population. After reunification, Gallier Hall was designated New Orleans's city hall and the Cabildo housed the state supreme court and the police department. Since 1911, when the state supreme court and the district police vacated the building, it has been part of the Louisiana State Museum. The mansard roof was added in 1847, echoing improvements being made in other properties along Jackson Square and rivaling Gallier Hall, then being erected in the American sector. The iron gateways and marble paving were added in the 1850s. Interior alterations, such as enlargement of the Sala Capitular on the second floor and removal of its original mantel (now replaced), had taken place earlier. Severely damaged by Hurricane Betsy in 1965, the building was renovated between 1966 and 1969 by Maxwell and Le Breton and Koch and Wilson.

1795–99. Gilberto Guillemard
Casa Capitular, New Orleans City Hall
711 Chartres Street (Orleans Parish)
National Historic Landmark

Wilmington Old Town Hall

Wilmington, Delaware

With its cupola and slightly projecting central three bays, topped by a pediment, Old Town Hall has the massing and silhouette common to municipal buildings of the second half of the 18th century. The building's limited but delicate detailing, such as the garlands in the cupola, place the building in the Federal style. Behind the tall, first-story windows are the stairway and a large assembly room, where Caesar Rodney and John Dickinson, signers of the Declaration of Independence, regularly met socially and where receptions for Andrew Jackson and Daniel Webster were held. The room was also used as a ballroom and as a meeting room for the U.S. District Court and such groups as the Philosophical Society, Abolition Society and Society of Free Masons. In 1875 two rear wings were erected and the cupola replaced with a much larger and more substantial fire tower. The rear wings served as the police headquarters and city prison, as these departments had outgrown the two basement cells originally provided. Other exterior details were replaced, reflecting changes in late 19th-century architectural tastes. When the city government moved to new facilities in 1916, the Old Town Hall Association purchased the building to prevent its demolition. Two restorations have been undertaken—one in 1926, under the direction of Edgar V. Seeler, and one in 1965, under the direction of the firm Whiteside Moeckel and Carbonell, with Lee Nelson and Henry Judd as consultants. The building, which is owned and operated by the Historical Society of Delaware, now serves as a colonial museum specializing in silver and furniture.

1798–1800. John Way and Peter Brynberg
House of Burgesses
512 Market Street Mall (New Castle County)
National Register of Historic Places

Charleston City Hall

Charleston, South Carolina

In spite of 19th-century political and architectural insensitivities, heavy Civil War shelling and severe earthquake and tornado damage, Charleston's city hall exemplifies the delicacy, stateliness and dignity of Federal-style architecture. These qualities suggest that the city hall was designed by Gabriel Manigault, whose graceful design of the Orphan House Chapel places him among Charleston's best architects. Built as the U.S. Bank Branch, the building served in that capacity until 1811, then as the State Bank from 1812 to 1818, when it became the city hall. Located on the public square, which has been the site of public markets since 1692, the building was drastically altered first in 1839, when a ceiling was added, dividing the first floor into two, and the interior partitioned. In 1882 the interior was gutted, the circular staircase removed and the exterior stuccoed, obliterating the contrast between the white-marble quoins and the red-brick walls laid in Flemish bond. Four years later an earthquake seriously damaged the masonry walls and those of the two-story council chamber. In 1938 a tornado blew off the roof and destroyed all the window panes. With the assistance of the Works Progress Administration (WPA), the city was able to repair and clean the building and its furnishings. The building's architecture is complemented by an art collection that includes a John Trumbull portrait of George Washington and a Samuel F. B. Morse portrait of James Monroe. Dignitaries such as Monroe, Lafayette and Secretary of War John C. Calhoun were guests at state dinners held in the city hall. The building still houses the mayor's office and various city staffs.

1800–01. Attributed to Gabriel Manigault
U.S. Bank Branch, State Bank of South Carolina
80 Broad Street (Charleston County)

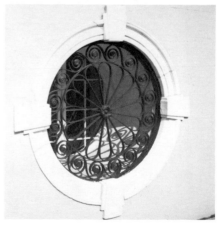

New York City Hall
New York, New York

In scale and some details, such as the cupola, this city hall reflects Federal-style characteristics, but its intricately detailed facade and balanced pavilions suggest the French Renaissance style. This French reinterpretation of classical architecture is marked by rounded openings, extensive detailing and precise balancing of wings. The symmetry extends to the interior, where the central rotunda's grand, divided staircase leads to the symmetrically arranged reception and meeting rooms and the Governor's Room. The room also contains the writing table used by President George Washington between April 1789 and August 1790, when New York City was the nation's capital. The architects were chosen by means of a design competition. The building represents the only collaboration between John McComb, the city's leading post-Revolutionary War architect, and Joseph Mangin, designer of the old St. Patrick's Cathedral and city surveyor who prepared the official city map published in 1803. Beneath the dome of the rotunda, the bodies of Abraham Lincoln and Ulysses S. Grant laid in state. The Governor's Room is decorated with 12 John Trumbull portraits commissioned by the city as early as 1790. Other distinguished American painters such as Samuel F. B. Morse, George Catlin, Eastman Johnson and Thomas Sully also are represented in the city hall's art collection. The structure occupies the northern end of a park that, at the time of its construction, marked the northern extent of settlement in New York City. The cupola has been destroyed twice by fire. In 1858 fireworks in celebration of the laying of the transatlantic cable ignited the tower; it was rebuilt according to architect Leopold Eidlitz's plan. After a 1917 fire it was reconstructed following the original design. A major interior renovation was carried out by Grosvenor Atterbury between 1908 and 1915. From 1954 to 1956, Shreve, Lamb and Harmon Associates replaced the deteriorated exterior marble and brownstone with white limestone and red granite.

1803–11. John McComb, Jr., and Joseph Francois Mangin
City Hall Park (New York County)
National Historic Landmark

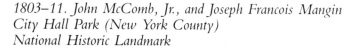

District of Columbia Old City Hall
Washington, D.C.

Like the Custis-Lee Mansion in Arlington, Va., also designed by George Hadfield, this building is a somewhat brutal execution of the Greek Revival style, now more notable for its siting than its architecture. The building's flat, undecorated wall expanses and simple columns typify the Greek Revival style. Hadfield, best known as a superintendent of construction for the U.S. Capitol, won the city hall project in a design competition. Construction was to have been financed by a lottery, but the manager absconded with the money; Congress stepped in to help the city finish the first section of the building. Although the central portion and east wing were finished in 1826, a lack of funds delayed final completion until 1849. A northern wing, connected to the main building by three wide hyphens, was added in 1881. The main facade of the building, with Lott Flannery's statue of Abraham Lincoln (1868) in front, forms a dramatic northern terminus for a vista starting at the Mall. Four 1930s buildings, built at the rear of the old city hall and reflecting its style, form two sides of a large "square" that is bordered on the south by the old city hall and on the north by the massive, red-brick Pension Building (1882–85, Montgomery C. Meigs). A succession of city, court and federal offices occupied the old city hall through the years until the federal government acquired it in 1873 for less than the District of Columbia government had paid for its construction. The building was restored in 1916, when the original stuccoed brick exterior was replaced by stone facing on brick, reinforced concrete and steel. At that time, the interior was rebuilt, featuring a "period" staircase and barrel-vaulted corridors on the lower level. The building was further altered in 1935 and 1966. It is now used by the District of Columbia's courts and police department.

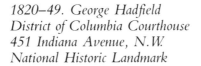

1820–49. George Hadfield
District of Columbia Courthouse
451 Indiana Avenue, N.W.
National Historic Landmark

Salem City Hall
Salem, Massachusetts

Salem, the second incorporated city in Massachusetts, built for its city hall a chaste Greek Revival structure with relief provided by carved decoration. Its wide pilasters and flat, largely undecorated surfaces are similar to those of America's most functional-looking and straightforward classical revival buildings. The one decorative element that is stylistically inconsistent is the Federal-style eagle above the parapet, supposedly a replica of one by Samuel McIntire, Salem's preeminent woodcarver and architect. The building's architect, Richard Bond, was a well-established Boston architect, best known for designing Lewis Wharf. Salem's first mayor, Leverett Saltonstall, was only one of Salem's mayors who went on to become prominent in state and national politics. In 1876 and 1976, additions were made to the rear of the building. The first one nearly doubled the size of the building, and the second provided additional fireproof vaults for city records.

1837–38. Richard Bond
93 Washington Street (Essex County)
National Register of Historic Places

Brooklyn City Hall
Brooklyn, New York

Considered one of New York's finest Greek Revival buildings, Brooklyn's borough hall embodies all the hallmarks of that style. The building's exquisite proportions, properly detailed ornamentation, chaste columns supporting the portico and bilateral symmetry belie the fact that it was designed by a carpenter-turned-architect. Located in a landscaped park, it is the oldest building in Brooklyn and has housed the borough's government since 1848. In the late 19th century, the cupola was rebuilt following a fire, stairs were removed from the two-story, colonnaded rotunda and others added at the building's eastern end, and the council chamber was reconstructed as a two-story courtroom with a coffered ceiling. Since the annexation of Brooklyn by New York City in 1898, the building has housed the borough president's offices.

1845–49. Gamaliel King
Brooklyn Borough Hall
209 Joralemon Street (Kings County)
National Register of Historic Places

Gallier Hall

New Orleans, Louisiana

An impressive example of classical revival architecture, Gallier Hall incorporates elements of ancient Roman and Greek architecture. The building has the appearance of a classical temple; its Ionic columns are supposedly based on those of the Temple Erechtheum in Athens. However, the high basement, or podium, and the sculpture within the pediment are characteristic of Roman architecture. This building is one of the last works of James Gallier, who was among the country's best classical revival architects. At the time of the building's construction, New Orleans was divided into three municipalities, with Gallier Hall serving as the municipal hall for the American sector. When the city was reunified in 1852, Gallier Hall, rather than the Cabildo, which served the Creole population, became New Orleans's city hall. The bodies of Jefferson Davis, president of the Confederate States of America, and Gen. Pierre G. T. Beauregard, who ordered the first shots of the Civil War to be fired, laid in state in Gallier Hall. The building faces Lafayette Square, which was landscaped in 1788. In 1908 an annex, connected by a pedestrian bridge to Gallier Hall, was erected. The building ceased to serve as New Orleans's city hall in 1957, but it still houses various city agencies and is also used for receptions and social functions. It was renovated by the city in 1969, but the Lyceum, a great meeting room on the third floor, was not restored because of the expense.

1845–50. James Gallier, Sr.
Municipal Hall, New Orleans City Hall
545 St. Charles Street (Orleans Parish)
National Historic Landmark

Knoxville City Hall

Knoxville, Tennessee

This building, originally constructed to house the Tennessee School for the Deaf, is one of the few remaining major Greek Revival structures in East Tennessee. After the Civil War, the school expanded rapidly; until 1899 additions and other major buildings were erected on the 11.5-acre site, reflecting the Italianate style and other styles popular during the period. In 1925, when the school vacated these buildings for a new complex, the city government bought the buildings and occupied them until 1980, when its offices moved to a new city-county building. Some secondary buildings have been demolished, and half the site was sold for a housing project for the elderly. The remaining six historic buildings are being sensitively rehabilitated by Anderson Notter Finegold for use by the Tennessee Valley Authority. An infill building, light wells and glass-enclosed pedestrian bridges to improve circulation also have been added. Some landscaping of the site, which overlooks downtown Knoxville, has been restored, and parking lots have been removed.

1846–52. Attributed to Jacob Newman
Tennessee School for the Deaf
Summit Hill Drive (Knox County)
National Register of Historic Places

Norfolk Old City Hall and Courthouse

Norfolk, Virginia

Shortly after Norfolk was chartered in 1845, the city advertised a design competition for a city hall and court building. The next year, the government selected a building site, having rejected arguments to build on the site of the old town hall, and chose William R. Singleton's classical revival design, which incorporated suggestions by Thomas U. Walter, architect of the U.S. Capitol extension. In 1860, from the steps of this city hall, presidential candidate Stephen Douglas addressed an unenthusiastic audience of an estimated 5,000 people. In 1918, when the Norfolk city government adopted the council-manager form, it moved its offices from this building to the city market (since demolished), which was used as the city hall until 1938. The original city hall continued to be used by the courts until 1960. From 1961 to 1963, the interior was gutted and rebuilt as a mausoleum; since 1964 it has been the tomb and museum for Gen. Douglas MacArthur, whose mother was a Norfolk native. The walls of six of the display rooms are covered by murals by Alton S. Tobey depicting the life of MacArthur, and in front of the building is a statue of MacArthur, a replica of that by Walter Hancock at the U.S. Military Academy at West Point.

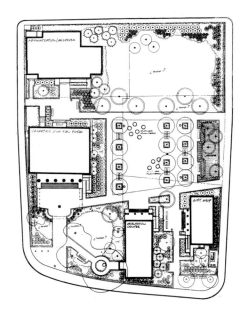

1847–50. William R. Singleton; Thomas U. Walter
General Douglas MacArthur Memorial
421 East City Hall Avenue
National Register of Historic Places

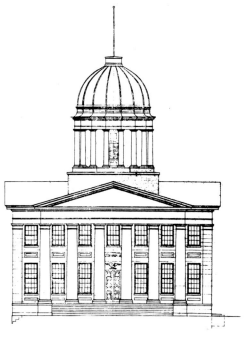

Mobile City Hall
Mobile, Alabama

This imposing Italianate structure demonstrates the ability of mid-19th-century architect-builders and clients to erect a suitably monumental building capable of serving a variety of purposes. Thomas S. James was a prominent Mobile builder and later architect who designed the Barton Academy and the Government Street Presbyterian Church. The municipal offices were located on the second floor, with the first floor housing an armory, a restaurant, several saloons and meat, produce and fruit markets. The building has undergone major interior changes including a 1938 WPA-financed conversion of some markets to office space. In September 1979, the building suffered substantial hurricane damage. Rehabilitation under the direction of Nicholas H. Holmes, Jr., FAIA, was completed in 1983, and the building is once again occupied by the city government.

1855–57. Thomas Simmons James
Southern Market and Municipal Building
107–115 South Royal Street (Mobile County)
National Historic Landmark

Wilmington City Hall/Thalian Hall
Wilmington, North Carolina

In exchange for the title to land held by the Thalian Association, Wilmington agreed to erect this structure combining a city hall and a theater. The verticality of its Italianate style, emphasized by the paired windows with hood moldings, is balanced by the horizontality of its cornice and classical portico. The latter, with its ornate capitals, is attributed to James Post, who was the builder of some of Wilmington's most important 19th-century buildings. In addition to the theater and city offices, the building has also housed a second-floor ballroom, which was later used as a library. Although the 20-foot-high first-floor corridors remain unchanged, partitions and new ceilings have been added to many rooms to create more work space. The first-floor council chamber is the only room that retains approximately its original height. Thalian Hall is one of the few surviving 19th-century theaters and was a model for the restoration of Ford's Theatre in Washington, D.C.

1855–58. J. M. Trimble and Company; James Francis Post
102 North Third Street (New Hanover County)
National Register of Historic Places

54

Petersburg City Hall

Petersburg, Virginia

Designed by Ammi B. Young, the first supervising architect of the U.S. Treasury Department, Petersburg's city hall is in the Second Renaissance Revival style Young favored for the numerous custom houses, post offices and courthouses he designed. Some of Young's best buildings include the courthouses in Boston and Windsor, Vt. This solid-looking structure was built for use as the city's custom house and post office. In 1938 it was adapted for use as Petersburg's city hall, with renovations financed by the WPA. Several interior changes and repairs were made in 1870, but the major alterations occurred in 1908–10, when three bays were added on the south facade. It was probably at this time that some of the window and door openings were changed, creating doors in the main facade's two central bays. The interior columns and staircases are original.

1856–59. Ammi B. Young
U.S. Custom House and Post Office
129–141 North Union Street
National Register of Historic Places

Boston Old City Hall

Boston, Massachusetts

Boston's old city hall is one of the first of many American buildings inspired by the new Louvre, constructed in Paris in 1854–80 during the French Second Empire, the reign of Napoleon III (1852–70). Architectural historian Marcus Whiffen credits this city hall with making the Second Empire style popular for American public buildings. This style is marked by a projecting central pavilion (and, usually, end pavilions), a dormered mansard roof and coupled columns and pilasters. The total effect is that of a complex but extremely well-integrated, three-dimensional facade and massing. Originally, the city intended to enlarge Charles Bulfinch's Suffolk County Court House, which was serving as the city hall, and went so far as to hold a design competition for the enlargement; however, the city then decided to demolish that building and erect on its site the design submitted by Gridley Bryant and Arthur Gilman. Both were successful Boston architects who collaborated from 1859 to 1866, when Gilman moved to New York. This city hall and its famous occupants, such as Mayor James Michael Curley, supposedly were the basis for Edwin O'Connor's novel *The Last Hurrah*. Located in the center of Boston's downtown, the building is adjacent to Peter Harrison's mid-18th-century King's Chapel and burying ground. In 1970 the building was renovated by Anderson Notter Associates for banking, office and restaurant use. At that time, the main staircase was removed, new levels were created and other interior changes were made. Previous changes included removal of some exterior ornamentation, alterations of the roof and its dormers and construction of a free-standing rear annex (1911). The building has been leased by the city to Architectural Heritage Foundation, a nonprofit developer, for 99 years. One of its occupants is the Northeast Regional Office of the National Trust for Historic Preservation.

1862–65. Gridley J. Fox Bryant and Arthur D. Gilman
41–45 School Street (Suffolk County)
National Historic Landmark

Salt Lake City Old City Hall

Salt Lake City, Utah

Serving as both a city hall and territorial capitol from 1866 until 1894, this building is closely identified with the struggles between the Mormon Church and the federal government over control of the Utah Territory. Occupation of the territory by the U.S. Army and the passage of federal laws prohibiting polygamy, limiting local court jurisdiction, dissolving the Mormon Church as a political body and requiring voter qualification oaths forced the territory to comply with the federal government. The building's architectural style does not conform to any of the then-popular styles. William Folsom, the Mormon Church's official architect and father of Brigham Young's 25th wife, used ornamentation in the stringcourses, cupola and cornice, but none of the detailing can be classified as a specific style. After the city and state government offices moved into other buildings, the city hall was occupied by the police department and, later, other municipal agencies. In 1961–62, the structure was dismantled, moved to a site opposite the state capitol and restored under the direction of Edward O. Anderson. Alterations through the years include the addition of a basement, platform, balustrades and louvers and replacement of the original roof. The building now houses the Utah Travel Council.

1864–66. William H. Folsom
Salt Lake City Council Hall
300 North State Street (Salt Lake County)
National Historic Landmark

Baltimore City Hall

Baltimore, Maryland

Baltimore had to hold three design competitions for its city hall. The winner of the first competition disappeared during the Civil War, the outcome of the second is unclear, and only two architects entered the third, with George A. Frederick emerging as the winner. This Second Empire–style building has the characteristic projecting pavilions and mansard roof, but the overly tall dome and the horizontally spreading mass it rests on appear imbalanced. Any awkwardness in proportions or detailing, however, is more than compensated for by such spaces as the multistory rotunda. Baltimore City Hall was Frederick's first commission and started him on a successful architectural career in the city. Baltimore is one of the first American cities to rehabilitate its city hall and use it for its original purpose. This rehabilitation, carried out during 1975–77 by Architectural Heritage–Baltimore and Meyers, D'Aleo and Patton, doubled the amount of floor space, improved circulation and created an art gallery, while restoring important public spaces such as the ceremonial room, rotunda and city council chamber. The ballroom, which may have been used in the 19th century as the armory, was divided into offices.

1867–75. George A. Frederick
100 North Holliday Street
National Register of Historic Places

60

Norwich City Hall

Norwich, Connecticut

Highly visible because of its tall tower and its elevated site, Norwich's city hall makes a grand statement appropriate for a building that has housed the county court, city offices, police department, jail, library and large town meeting room. At the time of the city hall's construction, Norwich was the state's fourth largest city, with several textile mills and stove and piston manufacturers. The building, designed by a local architectural firm, is characteristically Second Empire in style; the projecting and receding facade has at least four types of window moldings, complex and varied rooflines and ornate cornices and columns. The exterior grandeur extends to the interior, with its tall vestibule and large staircase. Many original furnishings and much interior decoration survive. A Second Empire–style rear addition was erected around 1909. The tower's clock and cupola probably date to the same period.

1870–73. Burdick and Arnold
Norwich Town Hall
Union Square (New London County)

Chicopee Old City Hall

Chicopee, Massachusetts

When Chicopee dedicated its city hall on December 21, 1871, the town's 72 young men who had died in the Civil War were foremost in the citizens' minds. The next day's paper described the ceremony and the building, which it characterized as "in the Byzantine style of architecture," and reprinted the full texts of memorial tablets on the building—name, date and location of death and, occasionally, cause ("disease contracted in prison"). Although local tradition holds that Ralph Waldo Emerson spoke at the dedication, he is not mentioned in the newspaper. Other prominent persons known to have appeared in the second-floor auditorium on other occasions include Horace Mann, Charles Dickens and Frederick Douglass. The building, which faces the historic center of Chicopee, originally housed the police department and library, as well as city offices. Charles Parker, of Boston, designed other buildings in Chicopee as well as Easthampton Town Hall and Holyoke City Hall. The building's architectural style is a composite of High Victorian Gothic elements (for example, the pointed arches and polychromy) and Romanesque Revival elements (for example, the arcaded corbel table), and through the years it has been little altered. Original black walnut and butternut woodwork remains, as do the leaded stained-glass windows. A four-story rear annex was erected in 1927.

1871. Charles Edward Parker
Market Square (Hampden County)
National Register of Historic Places

Louisville City Hall
Louisville, Kentucky

Louisville's city hall has several handsome features, none of which seems to fit with the others. The soaring clock tower with its mansard roof occupies the prominent corner location, but it bears little relationship to the building's lower three stories and clashes with the pediment above the entrance bays. This columned, projecting entrance and the flanking wall treatments have a dignity suggestive of the Renaissance Revival style. The animal heads above the second-story windows are fascinating bits of whimsy that perhaps indicate that the structure was built on a market site. The disparity of parts may simply reflect the fact that John Andrewartha won the city hall design competition with a Mr. Mergell, but the final plans were drawn up by Andrewartha and Stancliff and Company. Little is known about Andrewartha, although he is credited with designing several Louisville buildings and the state capitol annex in Frankfort. Following an 1875 fire, the tower was repaired and reconstructed; it was renovated during the period 1977–79. In 1906 an annex was built. Interior alterations were carried out during the late 1950s.

1870–73. John Andrewartha
601 West Jefferson Street (Jefferson County)
National Register of Historic Places

Alexandria City Hall

Alexandria, Virginia

This building was erected on the site designated for the market and city hall when Alexandria was founded in 1749. The tall, steepled tower, which seems out of place with the building's Second Empire–style massing and detailing, is a reconstruction of a tower designed by Benjamin H. Latrobe that was part of Alexandria's 1817 town hall. That hall burned in 1871, necessitating construction of the current building, designed by Adolph Cluss, a locally prominent architect who had designed Washington's Central Market in 1870. Originally, the city hall also housed the Masonic Lodge, court facility, police and fire stations and markets—stalls were located on the first floors of the west and north wings and in the courtyard— but only the city offices remain. On the southern half of the city hall block is a plaza completed in 1967. Through the years the structure has undergone several interior and exterior alterations, such as bricked-up openings. In the late 1940s, some interior renovation took place. The two most serious alterations occurred fairly recently. In 1960–61, the building's courtyard was used as the site for a Colonial Revival structure bearing no stylistic relationship to the city hall and very little, if any, to historic downtown Alexandria. Beginning in 1981, portions of the building's interior were gutted.

1871–73. Adolph Cluss
Alexandria Market House and City Hall
301 King Street

Philadelphia City Hall

Philadelphia, Pennsylvania

Philadelphians make staggering claims for their city hall: It is, they say, the nation's largest seat of municipal government, the highest occupied structure in the United States until 1909 and the world's tallest masonry-bearing structure. And it is an audacious example of Second Empire–style architecture, graced with magnificent, evocative sculpture by Alexander Calder, including a statue of William Penn atop the tower. The city hall occupies 4 acres in the center of the original city as laid out by Penn. Built to serve the needs of the consolidated governments of the city and county of Philadelphia, the structure has an equally staggering political history. Two competitions were held for the building—one in 1860 and one in 1868—and John McArthur, Jr., a Philadelphia architect and leading Second Empire–period architect, won both. Thomas U. Walter, who had been architect of the U.S. Capitol from 1851 until he resigned in 1865, served as consultant for the city hall and is credited with designing much of the detailing for the building. A dispute concerning the location for the building was resolved only by a referendum. During the course of construction, the state-appointed city hall building commission was ejected from the building by the mayor and police and restored only by order of the Pennsylvania Supreme Court. Rivalries between machine politicians so delayed the design and construction process that the building was not considered formally completed until 30 years after construction began. In the 1920s and 1930s, several schemes for demolition of the building and construction of a new city hall were suggested, including one by Paul Cret, FAIA, designer of the Folger Library, Washington, D.C. The city hall's exterior is unaltered, but the interior has undergone the alterations common to older government buildings, such as partitioning and the lowering of ceilings. Recently, the grand Conversation Hall was restored by Studio Four–Vitetta Group and is on view to the public for the first time in this century.

1871–1901. John McArthur, Jr., and Thomas U. Walter
The New Public Buildings
Penn Square (Philadelphia County)
National Historic Landmark

Providence City Hall

Providence, Rhode Island

The glory of Providence's city hall is not its competent, rather staid Second Empire–style exterior, but its interior spaces and details. The grandeur of the staircase is matched by the barrel-vaulted skylight 60 feet above and by the columns and elaborate balustrades flanking the stair court. Rooms such as the aldermen's chamber and the two-story council chamber are decorated with elaborate gold stenciling and light-colored wood; several doors have etched glass. Samuel Thayer obtained this commission in a design competition entered by several nationally prominent architects. The design proposed by Thayer, a Boston architect who never achieved a national reputation, won over the designs of two other finalists, although the judge said that none was "entirely suitable for a city hall without modification and amendment." The building faces a landscaped park. In 1914 the top floor was remodeled and some of the dormer windows altered. Irving B. Haynes and Associates, AIA, began renovating and restoring the building in 1980, including replicating the original color scheme and inventorying the historic furnishings.

1874–78. Samuel J. F. Thayer
West End of Kennedy Plaza (Providence County)
National Register of Historic Places

Lincoln Old City Hall

Lincoln, Nebraska

With its pointed-arch lintels and hipped, mansard roof, this building is partly High Victorian Gothic, partly Second Empire in style. It originally housed the post office, courthouse and U.S. Land Office, where between 1879 and 1906 Homestead Act claims for 5 million acres of land in southern Nebraska were filed. The building became Lincoln's first permanent city hall in 1907; previously, the city government had used rented offices. Designed by Alfred Mullett, supervising architect of the U.S. Treasury Department, the building's construction started during his tenure, a period marked by a large number of Second Empire–style federal buildings. Mullett's best designs as supervising architect were the Courthouse and Post Office (1866–69) in Springfield, Ill., and the Old State, War and Navy Building (1871–88) in Washington, D.C. In 1875, William Potter, known for his High Victorian Gothic architecture, replaced Mullett and redesigned the building. To what degree he modified Mullett's design is not clear. Potter served only two years as supervising architect, and his best work was done while he was in private architectural practice. His powerful High Victorian Gothic buildings often show the influence of H. H. Richardson. The building was first renovated in 1906–07, when it was converted for use as the city hall. In 1978 restoration was begun, and the building is now being used by civic groups. Once the building was the only structure on a large green, in the center of blocks of commercial architecture. The green has virtually disappeared, replaced with buildings and parking spaces.

1874–79. Alfred B. Mullett; William A. Potter
U.S. Post Office and Courthouse
916 O Street (Lancaster County)
National Register of Historic Places

Flatbush Town Hall

Brooklyn, New York

This High Victorian Gothic–style building was constructed following the defeat of a referendum to annex Flatbush to the city of Brooklyn. Flatbush having retained its independence, the local newspapers then successfully campaigned for the town to build its own town hall. The tower, gables and pointed-arched openings exaggerate the building's height and are partially countered by the horizontal moldings (which are continuous on the first floor), date panels and banding. The most attractive feature of this building—and the most familiar characteristic of the High Victorian Gothic style—is the polychromatic surface. Warm orange and red-brick walls are contrasted with lighter brownstone moldings. The interior's most interesting feature is the large ballroom. Flatbush Town Hall is the only known building by John Cuyler, an engineer, who is remembered for his involvement in the construction of Brooklyn's Prospect Park. After Flatbush was finally annexed by Brooklyn in 1894, the building later housed the courts and police department. In 1929–30 a rear addition was erected for the homicide court. After being vacated in 1972, the town hall was slated for demolition for a parking lot but was saved by the efforts of a citizens group. The building has been renovated for use as a community center.

1875. John Yapp Cuyler
35 Snyder Avenue (Kings County)
National Register of Historic Places

Albany City Hall

Albany, New York

"In her city hall, Albany rejoices in what is one of the most beautiful exteriors in America," declared a 1891 guidebook to Albany. "It is to be doubted whether there is another municipal building in which so much taste is displayed. It is the work of the late Mr. H. H. Richardson, probably the greatest American architect of his time, and it is said he regarded it as one of his best designs." The structure, which was built to house city and county governments, is vintage Richardson in the use of contrasting colors, rough facing, varied sizes of stone and "Syrian" arches. Most important, it has the rugged, balanced strength typical of Richardson's architecture. His influence was so pervasive—witness the many Richardsonian Romanesque–style city halls and state capitols throughout the country—that he is one of the few architects to have a style named after him. Across from this building is the New York State Capitol (1867–99), of which he was also one of the principal architects, along with Thomas Fuller, Leopold Eidlitz and Isaac Perryl. The 1891 description praises only the building's exterior. Because of budget constraints, the interiors were not executed according to Richardson's design and were undistinguished; they were redesigned in 1919 by Ogden and Gander. The design of the courtrooms and offices is vaguely Georgian Revival, while the corridors are in a colder, Beaux-Arts style. In 1926 a carillon was installed as a memorial to World War I soldiers. Five murals, painted in 1971 and 1972, commemorate events in American history. The building continues to serve the city government, although the county offices were moved in 1916.

1881–83. Henry Hobson Richardson
Eagle Street (Albany County)
National Register of Historic Places

Hoboken City Hall

Hoboken, New Jersey

Built on the site of the city market, the city hall designed for Hoboken by Francis Himpler was a flat, vitiated rendering of the Second Empire style. The building was constructed one year after the New Jersey legislature authorized cities that lacked city halls, such as Hoboken, to erect one on city-held or donated public land. Himpler, a German-born architect, is remembered for his church designs in Kansas, New York, New Jersey, Missouri and Ohio. The 1912–13 renovation added wings and gave the facade a monumental appearance. The change was dramatic, producing a Beaux-Arts structure with symmetry, depth and a ceremonial quality reflecting the style popularized by the 1893 World's Columbian Exposition in Chicago. The remodeled building also contained the police department, jail and district court, and its third floor housed an armory and an exhibition area. As Hoboken was a major embarkation port for World War I troops, the armory was extensively used. Also during that period, the city hall was beseiged by troops trying to free their comrades incarcerated in the city hall jail. In 1976 the building was renovated and the masonry cleaned. However, serious spalling of the brownstone continues.

1881–83. Francis George Himpler. 1912–13. Schneider and Dieffenback
86–98 Washington Street (Hudson County)
National Register of Historic Places

New Britain City Hall

New Britain, Connecticut

Joseph Wells, a short-lived star in the nationally prominent firm of McKim, Mead and White, is credited with designing this Second Renaissance Revival–style hotel and office building for two of New Britain's prominent hardware manufacturers, Henry Russell and Cornelius Erwin. Despite the overhang, roundheaded windows and arcading, the building lacks the dignity of the firm's other designs in this style, such as the Villard Houses (1882–86), New York City; they also were designed by Wells. Although initially successful, the hotel did not prosper, and in 1908–09 the building was converted by the same firm into New Britain's first city hall; previously, the city had rented offices in this building. The structure is in the center of the city, opposite a park with architect Ernest Flagg's Civil War monument. In the late 19th century, the building was enlarged by three rear additions.

1884–85. McKim, Mead and White
Russell and Erwin Building, Russwin Hotel
27 West Main Street (Hartford County)
National Register of Historic Places

Lawrence City Hall

Lawrence, Kansas

Built as a bank and mortgage office for J. B. Watkins, who provided mortgages for hundreds of thousands of acres of farm land in six midwestern and western states, this structure was bequeathed by Watkins's widow for use as the city hall. In accordance with the provisions that it not house the fire department and jail, it served as the city hall from 1929 to 1970. Although the building incorporates such Richardsonian motifs as the rough-faced stone arch, banding and arcaded windows, it lacks the vigor of Richardson's own works. Walter Root was apparently sent to Kansas City in 1885 to supervise the Kansas projects of his older brother's firm, Burnham and Root. Walter is credited with independently designing buildings at the University of Kansas as well as Lawrence City Hall. The structure is opposite the county courthouse, built on land donated by Mrs. Watkins, and both buildings border a landscaped park. Since 1975 the Douglas County Historical Society has owned the building and used it to house a community museum, the Kansas All Sports Hall of Fame and historical society offices.

1885–88. Walter Root
J. B. Watkins Land Mortgage Company and Bank Building, Elizabeth M. Watkins Community Museum
1047 Massachusetts Street (Douglas County)
National Register of Historic Places

Rochester City Hall

Rochester, New York

Rochester's city hall, built as a U.S. post office and courthouse, is one of those rare buildings that is equally impressive on the inside and on the outside, although the two are quite different. Richardsonian in its rough-faced stone, arcaded windows and massive corner tower, this building anchors the intersection and has a presence perhaps equaling Richardson's Albany City Hall. In contrast, the interior's cortile projects a sense of lightness, luxurious materials and sophistication. Harvey Ellis, a nationally prominent architect who was a Rochester native, is often credited with designing this building, although Mifflin Bell, the supervising architect of the U.S. Treasury Department from 1883 until 1887, has also been credited with the design. In cooperation with the Landmark Society of Western New York, the U.S. General Services Administration delayed selling or demolishing this building until it was purchased by the city for one dollar in 1975. From 1976 to 1978, the architectural firm of Handler and Grosso renovated and restored the building, adding a four-story addition. Between the original building and the new addition is a one-story addition, built around 1910. In May 1978, six years after the federal agencies vacated this building for a new facility, the former post office and courthouse was dedicated as Rochester's city hall.

1884–91. Harvey Ellis or Mifflin E. Bell
U.S. Post Office and Court House
30 Church Street (Monroe County)
National Register of Historic Places

Richmond Old City Hall
Richmond, Virginia

Massive, busy and audacious, Richmond's city hall could have been designed only in the late 19th century. On the exterior, the rough-faced stone competes with a plethora of window and portal details, roof dormers, corner towers of varying heights and an elaborate skylight, yet all these elements coalesce. The exterior is rivaled by the interior, with its bizarrely decorated columns, Gothic trim, striking skylight, two cortiles and grand staircase. Gothic-arched arcades surround the courtyards of the city hall, which overlooks the state capitol, designed by Thomas Jefferson. The history of the building's design is as complex as its architecture. Elijah Myers won the first city hall design competition, although the cost of his building would have exceeded the specified limit. He lost the second competition, and the winner prepared working drawings, but the building committee awarded Myers the commission. Understandably, the winner of the second competition sued, but only for services rendered, and Myers was investigated for bribery. Budgeted at $300,000, the building ultimately cost $1.3 million. Myers also designed numerous county courthouses, the Michigan State Capitol (1872–79), Texas State Capitol (1883–88) and Colorado State Capitol (1890–94). Despite his numerous important commissions, he gained an unsavory reputation because of the Richmond City Hall and other projects that were over budget. The city hall has been restored and leased for luxury office space.

1886–94. Elijah E. Myers
Courts Building
1001 East Broad Street
National Historic Landmark

Springfield Old City Hall
Springfield, Ohio

Springfield had planned to raze this building for a new municipal center, but its inclusion in the National Register of Historic Places, through the efforts of the Clark County Historical Society, dissuaded the city government. Instead, this Richardsonian Romanesque hulk, which originally had a large farmers market, opera house and city offices (including the police department and, possibly, the fire department), now houses a much smaller farmers market, the Ohio Baseball Hall of Fame and a city storage area. In 1914 the International City Management Association was formed here. The architect, Charles Cregar, was, with his father and brother, a partner in Springfield's most successful architectural firm. Occupying a long narrow lot, the building has a five-part, symmetrical side elevation. The interior has been substantially altered with the partitioning of major spaces such as the market, opera house and council chamber. The caps of the towers have been removed and some openings filled. Original details—colorful tiles, fluted Corinthian iron columns and carved oak beams—remain in the area that housed the farmers market.

1888–90. Charles A. Cregar
City Building, Municipal Building
117 South Fountain Avenue (Clark County)
National Register of Historic Places

San Antonio City Hall

San Antonio, Texas

Situated in the center of a plaza that has been the seat of government since the 18th century, San Antonio's city hall is now bereft of its most interesting features. When a fourth floor was added in 1927, the domed, octagonal clock tower and conical and mansard-roof corner towers—there were apparently two of each—were removed. Both entrances to the building now have 1920s Spanish Colonial Revival–style door enframements. At least one of them replaced a two-level, columned portico with a balcony, whose balustrade balanced one at roof level that was removed in 1927. The building's eastern facade faces an 18th-century church, while the western facade overlooks a mid-19th-century Spanish governor's palace. The construction of the city hall on Military Plaza ended the open-air market and social activities that had traditionally taken place there. The architect, Otto Kramer, was from St. Louis and was well known for his designs throughout the Midwest.

1888–91. Otto Kramer
Military Plaza (Bexar County)

Cincinnati City Hall

Cincinnati, Ohio

This building, considered Cincinnati's best extant Richardsonian Roman-esque–style structure, is a bold, powerful articulation of that style by an important and prolific Ohio architect. Samuel Hannaford's firm is credited with designing more than 300 buildings in Ohio, Kentucky, Indiana, West Virginia and Tennessee. With its massive center pavilion and corner clock tower, the building dominates the intersection of Plum and Eighth streets with two other architectural masterpieces—St. Peter-in-Chains Cathedral (1841–45, Thomas U. Walter) and Isaac M. Wise Temple (1865–66, James Wilson). Alterations include filling in of some windows and replacement of the sash in all windows. Roof cresting and several finials have been removed, although the latter are being duplicated. The replastering of ceilings and walls has obscured the original wallpaper and murals by F. Pedretti's Sons, with the exception of one ceiling mural in the east foyer.

1888–93. Samuel Hannaford
801 Plum Street (Hamilton County)
National Register of Historic Places

Cambridge City Hall
Cambridge, Massachusetts

This Richardsonian Romanesque–style building is situated on a slight rise on Cambridge's main thoroughfare. Cambridge's most impressive civic building, the city hall was designed by a local firm specializing in revival style and Shingle Style residences. The building was donated by Frederick Rindge, a local philanthropist who sponsored the design competition. The joined, round-arched windows and the contrast between the beige granite walls and brownstone trim are typical Richardsonian motifs, but the relationship between the tower and lower stories, because of the difference in scale, is awkward. The building's solidity, siting, attractive colors and fine detailing in the tower and dormers more than compensate for its awkwardness. The city hall is largely unaltered, although some rooms have been partitioned. Despite the alterations, the interiors have the detailing and warm colors characteristic of Richardsonian designs. Especially handsome are the substantial chimney breasts and beautifully carved wooden furniture.

1889. Longfellow, Alden and Harlow
795 Massachusetts Avenue (Middlesex County)

Syracuse City Hall

Syracuse, New York

The March 11, 1892, edition of the Syracuse *Evening News*, in a long, laudatory article on the new city hall, praised the building as the most unified and excellent of Richardsonian Romanesque seen by the journalist. It was, he wrote, "a structure which has taken form and proportion by degrees until the whole stands to-day an exemplification of man's genius and creative ability. . . . Solid without being heavy and light without proving flimsy, it promises to be not only durable and useful but ornamental as well." A nonpartisan commission chose Charles Colton, a Syracuse native, to be the architect for the city hall building. Originally housing the police department as well as city offices, the building also provided a public hall, or assembly hall. Built one block from the Erie Canal, the city hall is on the site of its predecessor, a market converted to city offices in the mid–19th century. In 1977 the architectural firm of Quinlivan, Pierik and Krause renovated the building, restoring the council chamber and other original features. The skylight was closed early in the century.

1889–92. Charles Erastus Colton
233 East Washington Street (Onondaga County)
National Register of Historic Places

Lewiston City Building

Lewiston, Maine

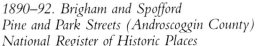

After Lewiston's 1870s Gothic Revival-style city hall burned in 1890, a new city hall was erected on the same site. The new structure has overtones of the Italian Renaissance style, especially in the tower's dome and the third-floor Palladian windows. These windows originally illuminated a large, 32-foot-high public meeting hall with a stage and balconies on three sides. Although the architectural style was changed, both buildings had approximately the same massing, with the middle bays of the two major facades being prominent. This emphasis was reinforced in the later structure by erecting the tower over the center bays of the Pine Street facade rather than at the corner, as was the case with the preceding building, thus giving the new structure a different orientation. Charles Brigham and John Calvin Spofford were Boston architects whose most important commission was probably the extension of the Massachusetts State House. They designed several town and city halls throughout New England.

1890–92. Brigham and Spofford
Pine and Park Streets (Androscoggin County)
National Register of Historic Places

Minneapolis City Hall and Courthouse

Minneapolis, Minnesota

This building has been characterized by architectural historian Marcus Whiffen as an imitation of H. H. Richardson's Allegheny County Courthouse in Pittsburgh. This comparison, however, does not do justice to the structure, which expresses Richardson and the era's sense of manifest destiny. It is massive, occupying an entire block, with wide, large corner pavilions, monumental towers above the two entrances and the heavy, rough-faced stone typically used in Richardsonian arches and walls. As rough as the exterior is, the interior is polished and refined. The major feature is a five-story gray marble cortile, topped by a marble ceiling with a stained-glass skylight. In the center of the rotunda is Larkin Mead's sculpture *Mississippi—Father of Waters*; behind the sculpture are the marble stairs that divide when they reach the back wall, which has a three-part stained-glass window. Built jointly as a city-county venture, with the commission going to the winner of a design competition, the building not only housed county courts and city offices, including the police and fire departments; it also included public spaces such as the Grand Army of the Republic Hall, Ladies Hall, Public Assembly and a three-story council chamber. Long and Kees was a Minneapolis architectural firm that also designed the Lumber Exchange, Corn Exchange, Masonic Temple and Public Library in Minneapolis. All the building's larger spaces have been subdivided, and in 1949 a four-story building was erected in the interior courtyard. Additional changes have included lowering ceilings and changing openings.

1889–1905. Long and Kees
Municipal Building
350 South Fifth Street (Hennepin County)
National Register of Historic Places

Lowell City Hall

Lowell, Massachusetts

The city of Lowell is internationally known as the model for the enlightened 19th-century mill town. The mill owners, who founded and controlled Lowell in the early 19th century, believed correctly that they could attract an efficient work force of farmers' daughters by providing proper housing. By the time this second city hall was erected, the mills were past their peak, dependent on immigrant labor, and the mill owners' control of the city had waned. Thus, Lowell City Hall can be seen not only as a well-executed Richardsonian Romanesque city hall but also as a declaration of the city government's new-found independence from the mill owners. Perhaps reflecting the government's uneasy first steps, the competition for the city hall was mishandled: The winner did not get the commission. It went to the third-prize winner, although the first-prize winner did get to design the adjacent memorial hall–city library. The city hall faces Monument Square (actually a triangle), where several Civil War and World War I memorial sculptures are displayed. The building's interior and furnishings are intact. Especially pleasing are the carved fireplaces and mantels, stained glass and decoration of the council chamber.

1890–93. Merrill and Cutler
407 Merrimack Street (Middlesex County)
National Register of Historic Places

90

St. Louis City Hall
St. Louis, Missouri

George Mann, the winner of a national design competition for St. Louis City Hall, had been trained in the Beaux-Arts style at the Massachusetts Institute of Technology. He submitted a design in the French Renaissance Revival style, an especially appropriate choice for a city so proud of its French heritage. Harvey Ellis was a draftsman in Mann's firm, Eckel and Mann, and is thought to have played a major role in the design of the city hall. Albert Groves, of the firm of Weber and Groves, was brought in to ensure the building's completion in time for the 1904 St. Louis World's Fair. The rhythm of the projecting pavilions, high hipped roofs and tall dormers was even more lively before the removal in 1936 of the lanternlike central tower and flanking spires. The central, square, four-story atrium with its divided staircase projects a sense of grandeur that has seldom been equaled in municipal architecture. This space is lighted by a skylight surrounded by ribs with stenciled patterns. Other rooms also have interesting decorations: The board of aldermen's chamber has murals by C. Arthur Thomas of New York City depicting prominent St. Louis residents, and the chamber of the board of public service has five murals by William W. Davis of St. Louis, representing Time, Justice and Victory and the seals of Missouri and St. Louis. In 1896 the Republican National Convention was held in a temporary facility on the grounds adjacent to the city hall and nominated William McKinley as its presidential candidate. Other than the removal of the tower and spires, the building has undergone few alterations.

1890–1904. George Richard Mann; Harvey Ellis; Albert B. Groves
Tucker Boulevard at Market Street

Lancaster Municipal Building

Lancaster, Pennsylvania

Built as a post office, this structure, with its prominent corner tower and the juxtaposition of highly eclectic details, makes a bold statement of federal presence in Lancaster—which was perhaps the client's intent. Defying any meaningful stylistic characterization, the building is a strong, compelling, somewhat jarring piece of architecture. In 1907–08 substantial rear additions, designed by C. Emlen Urban and James Knox Taylor, supervising architect of the U.S. Treasury Department, were built. In 1931, when the building was converted for use as the city hall, the interior was remodeled, and details such as the barrel-vaulted ceiling in the foyer were added.

1891–92. James H. Windrim
U.S. Post Office
120 North Duke Street (Lancaster County)

New Whatcom City Hall

Bellingham, Washington

Built on a bluff overlooking Bellingham Bay, this structure was conceived as a symbol of New Whatcom, formed in 1891 by the merger of two towns. Choice of the site was deliberate: According to the January 15, 1892, New Whatcom city council minutes, "This location with this building constructed thereon would be the first attraction of strangers coming into our harbor and a sure index to all newcomers, tourists and travelers of our taste, thrift, enterprise, and intelligence." Eleven years later, New Whatcom merged with another town, and this building became the Bellingham City Hall. Even if it had not been built on a hill, the structure would have been easily visible because of its high roofs, corner towers and large central tower. The architect, Alfred Lee, had worked as a wagon maker in Oregon, but when he moved to Bellingham Bay in 1890, he opened an architectural office. The building became a museum in 1939, when a new city hall was built. The tower was destroyed in a 1962 electrical fire but was restored when the museum was remodeled from 1966 to 1974. The original jail and police department offices, once located in the basement, are no longer in the building, but the two-story height and balcony of the former council chamber have been retained.

1892–93. Alfred Lee
Bellingham City Hall, Bellingham Public Museum,
Whatcom Museum of History and Art
121 Prospect Street (Whatcom County)
National Register of Historic Places

Salt Lake City City and County Building
Salt Lake City, Utah

Occupying one of the city's most historic sites, this mammoth structure is another variation on the Richardsonian Romanesque style. It was erected to replace the inadequate facilities occupied by the city and county governments. The result of the second design competition for a joint city-county building, it has the rough-faced, variegated surface treatment and rounded arches that H. H. Richardson favored. The columns and tower are unusually elongated, creating an excessive vertical emphasis; hence, the building seems less earthbound than Richardson's own masterpieces. Monheim, Bird and Proudfoot was a short-lived Salt Lake City architectural firm. Founded in 1891, it was dissolved after the death in 1893 of Henry Monheim, supposedly Salt Lake City's most prolific architect. Bird and Proudfoot later collaborated in the design of Des Moines City Hall (1910–11). In addition to serving local governments, the Salt Lake City building also functioned as the state capitol until 1915, when the current capitol building was constructed. The site, one of the city's four original squares, was first used for cattle drives, a hay market and public entertainment. The grounds are planted with 45 varieties of trees brought by the Mormon settlers. Earthquakes and severe weathering of the sandstone exterior led to the removal of most of the iron and stone sculpture at the building's roofline. The building's exterior has been restored. On the interior, a light well has been closed and other alterations have been made.

1892–94. Monheim, Bird and Proudfoot
451 Washington Street (Salt Lake County)
National Register of Historic Places

Portland City Hall

Portland, Oregon

Considered the most important work by Whidden and Lewis, Portland's most important architectural firm during this period, this city hall is a pleasing, small-scale Second Renaissance Revival–style palace. The original plans included a tower, which was never erected. The building was not intended to house the police department and jail, but its third floor was used by a museum and a historical society until the 1930s, when the city reclaimed the space. The curved, three-story portico and stylized banding of the free-standing columns and lower floors give this building a verve that is often lacking in the better known Second Renaissance Revival–style works of McKim, Mead and White, the former employers of William Whidden and Ion Lewis. Portland City Hall was the first important commission for Whidden and Lewis. This tradition of giving commissions that launch major architects was most recently continued in the city's selection of Michael Graves to design the recently completed Portland Municipal Building. The city hall has undergone the usual interior alterations such as partitioning and remodeling of the council chamber. In the 1960s, the portico was reconstructed following a bombing incident.

1892–95. Whidden and Lewis
1220 S.W. Fifth Avenue (Multnomah County)
National Register of Historic Places

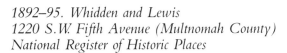

Brockton City Hall

Brockton, Massachusetts

The local newspaper's obituary of architect Wesley Minor described him as "about [as] forceful a citizen as Brockton had when in his prime, widely known, positive in his convictions, ready to fight for them, as ready to defend any cause which commended itself to him as worthy. . . . Mr. Minor builded well when Brockton accepted his plans for its city hall—and collected to the last dollar what he deemed was his rightful and fairly earned compensation." Minor demonstrated his feistiness three years before construction began, when he accused the city government of using his drawings of the proposed city hall as the basis for a city hall building competition that was, in his opinion, rigged so that he could not win. Somehow he did win and continued to argue with the government, even after the building was completed, over liability for supposed building defects. The structure, like Minor, has a certain directness. It is symmetrically organized around a central corridor that runs from the west entrance approximately two-thirds the length of the building, where it terminates in an octagonal rotunda. The corridor and rotunda were intended as memorials to the Civil War dead and are decorated with plaques and paintings of Civil War battle scenes. From the rotunda, cross corridors lead to the south and north entrances. The eastern opening off the rotunda leads into the public library, which is articulated on the building's exterior by the rounded facade at the eastern end. The extensive decoration—on the cornice, the keystones, stringcourse, chimney stacks and, especially, the clock tower—suggests a desire on the architect's part to move beyond the Richardsonian Romanesque style, with its emphasis on texture, massing and polychromy, to a more ornamental style. The building's ornamentation seems closer to the work of Louis Sullivan or to the more picturesque style of Richard Morris Hunt. Following a 1957 fire, the rotunda, which was open to the second floor, was closed and the coffered ceiling in the monumental hallway was covered. The architectural firm Endevor renovated the building during 1977–79. At that time the oak window and door frames were replaced with bronze-colored metal ones.

1892–94. Wesley Lyng Minor
45 School Street (Plymouth County)
National Register of Historic Places

Las Vegas City Hall

Las Vegas, New Mexico

This squat, vernacular interpretation of the Richardsonian Romanesque style has certain idiosyncrasies such as the stringcourses, pedimented lintels, bracketed overhang and eagles flanking the entrance arch. Three explanations can be offered for the unusual detailing: The architects had limited knowledge of the Richardsonian Romanesque style, or they were so familiar with it that they were searching for an alternative, or the detailing was influenced by the masons who constructed the building. H. M. Kirchner and A. H. Kirchner were St. Louis architects with a branch office in Denver, so it is most likely that they were thoroughly versed in the Richardsonian idiom. The daughter of the head of the masonry firm, F. Pettine and Sons, credits the look of the city hall to her father. Built to serve as the town hall and fire department, it also provided temporary space for the high school and, until 1904, the first library, run by the Women's Christian Temperance Union. Since 1964 it has housed only the fire and police departments. The interior was renovated in 1937 by the WPA, and a one-story garage was added in the late 1940s.

1892–96. Kirchner and Kirchner
Las Vegas City Police and Fire Department
626 Sixth Street (San Miguel County)

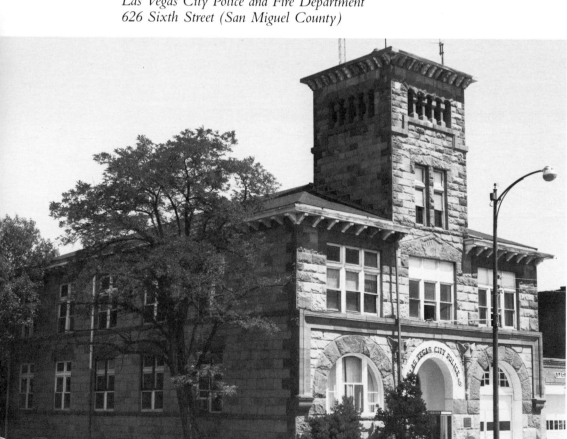

Bay City City Hall
Bay City, Michigan

At the building's dedication on March 22, 1897, Mayor Hamilton M. Wright declared that the new city hall was one of the finest examples of Richardsonian Romanesque–style public buildings: "Beautiful in conception, artistic and finished to its smallest detail, convenient in arrangement, and admirably adapted to every need of the public service, it leaves nothing to be desired." The features that prompted such praise included the landmark clock tower, the four-story staircase with ornate metal balustrade and columns lighted by a skylight, the oak paneling and the three-story council chamber. In 1889 Bay City was experiencing a boom economy, and the city leaders decided that the current city hall would be inadequate to meet projected needs. By the time the architects submitted plans, in 1892, the boom had collapsed, and the project went ahead as it was intended only as a stimulus to the economy. The city council required that all workers on the project be from Bay City and that local materials be used. Leverett A. Pratt and Walter Koeppe were local architects who designed numerous public buildings and churches in Michigan. From 1977 to 1980, $3.1 million was spent for the restoration of the building under the direction of architect John T. Meyer.

1894–97. Pratt and Koeppe
301 Washington Avenue (Bay County)

Milwaukee City Hall

Milwaukee, Wisconsin

Designed and built by German-born Americans for a city with a large German-American population, Milwaukee's city hall is thought to bear more than a casual resemblance to German town halls of the same period. The building was erected on the site of the old market hall, which had been used as city offices, but only after protracted disagreements concerning site and architect selection. For eight years Milwaukee's three wards battled to be the site for the city hall. It took 29 ballots by the city council to reach an agreement on the building site. Henry Koch was declared the winner of the national design competition only after the choice of the majority of jurors was rejected and a compromise collapsed. Koch, who was brought as an infant to Milwaukee from Germany, developed a successful regional architectural practice specializing in public buildings. The great height and vertical emphasis of the clock tower, resting on its massive arches, is echoed by the eight-story hexagonal light well in the interior. The exterior is largely unaltered, although all the interior spaces have been modified.

1893–95. Henry C. Koch and Company
200 East Wells Street (Milwaukee County)
National Register of Historic Places

Alameda City Hall

Alameda, California

At present, this building is less picturesque and serves fewer city agencies than when it was completed. The distressing change in the building's appearance is the loss of the central clock tower with its loggia and balcony. A 1906 earthquake damaged the tower, and the loggia portion was removed; the remainder of the tower was torn down in 1937. The tower's height and detailing brought life to the facade; the remaining features—overhangs, exterior stairs and entrance loggia—lack sufficient vigor to make the building exciting. Twenty-seven firms entered the design competition for the project, but only Percy and Hamilton submitted detailed price estimates; this information persuaded the cost-conscious city trustees that the structure could be built for the allocated amount. Percy and Hamilton designed 200 buildings in the San Francisco Bay Area, including the Stanford University art museum and Children's Playhouse in Golden Gate Park. Originally, the entire first-floor wing was used as a library and the basement as the police department, jail and court. The library moved out in 1902, and the police department, jail and court moved in 1978.

1895–96. Percy and Hamilton
2329 Santa Clara Avenue (Alameda County)
National Register of Historic Places

Peoria City Hall

Peoria, Illinois

Peoria's city hall is organized around a four-story atrium and staircase, lighted by a stained-glass skylight. This central plan is evident on the exterior by the cupola, placement of roof dormers and the symmetrical, recessed light wells on the two side elevations. All the facades are characterized by the use of rough- and smooth-faced stones, although there is a discernible hierarchy. The front facade has a round-arched entrance bay as well as three roof dormers, with the large central dormer lined up over the entrance. The side elevations have the same entrances as the main facade but are less important, for their central roof dormers and bays have been eliminated to create light wells. The rear facade lacks an entrance, dormers and the pronounced division of the wall into bays. A new civic center by Johnson and Burgee flanks three sides of the building and heightens the original emphasis on its main facade. The interior features leaded-glass windows and some murals.

1897–98. Reeves and Bailee
419 Fulton Street (Peoria County)
National Register of Historic Places

Binghamton Old City Hall

Binghamton, New York

A December 1970 report by the Binghamton Commission on Architecture and Urban Design concluded that the future character and personality of downtown Binghamton would be determined largely by the preservation of the current city hall. At that time, a new city hall was under construction as part of a government center; the report contended that the old city hall, a Beaux-Arts masterpiece, and an adjacent county courthouse offered a historical and architectural counterbalance to the new complex being erected only a few blocks away. The old city hall, whose third and fourth floors housed a two-story council chamber and a monumental interior staircase, demonstrates how successfully an architect trained at the Ecole des Beaux-Arts, Raymond Francis Almirall, could create grandeur. As with several city halls of this period, the architect was chosen on the basis of a design competition. Ingle and Almirall was a New York City architectural firm best known for its institutional buildings in New York State. Although not a large building, the city hall had a large public hall, space for the police department and courts and a tall, open cupola supposedly based on the cupola of Paris's city hall, the Hotel de Ville. In May 1983, 11 years after the city government vacated the building, it reopened as a luxury hotel, appropriately named the Hotel de Ville.

1897–98. Ingle and Almirall
Collier Street (Broome County)
National Register of Historic Places

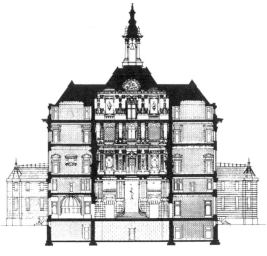

Lafayette Old City Hall

Lafayette, Louisiana

Although chartered in 1824, Lafayette did not have its own city hall until 1906, when it acquired a bank building for this use. Apparently, the founders of the Bank of Lafayette believed that a bank building need not look staid or conservative. Instead of the classical revival facades then in vogue for large urban banks, Lafayette's had a busy assortment of shapes, indentations, projections and decorations. George Knapp, one of Lafayette's earliest architects and the city building inspector, learned his profession through a mail-order course. In addition to city agencies, the city hall also housed Lafayette's first library, organized by a women's club, on the first floor. Although a new city hall was erected with federal funds in 1939, city agencies have continued to use the building. Rear jail cells, constructed in 1908, were demolished in 1959. The building has been renovated by the architect M. L. Boulet for occupancy by the Council for the Development of French in Louisiana.

1898. George Knapp
Bank of Lafayette
217 West Main Street (Lafayette Parish)

Creston Municipal Complex
Creston, Iowa

This formidable building, built as a railroad station, recalls the glory of turn-of-the-century American railroading, when the country's most eminent architects—H. H. Richardson, McKim, Mead and White, and Burnham and Root—designed depots. During its prime, around 1910, this station served 24 passenger trains daily. The steep, hipped roof and dormers balance the long mass of the building. The facades have a minimum of surface decoration, but the round-arched openings and banding lend the structure a solidness and probity well suited for both the railroad business and municipal functions. The large waiting room, now the memorial room, with its polished masonry and wood panels and coffered ceiling, reinforces this sense of appropriateness. The juxtaposition of the white, rounded columns with large Ionic capitals and the dark, coffered wood ceiling seems to anticipate the postmodern movement in architecture. The 1979 restoration and conversion of the station by Wagner, Marquart, Wetherall and Ericsson for use as municipal offices, public meeting rooms and dining space for the elderly has been cited by the Iowa State Historical Department as a model of adaptive use. The project was funded by a local bond issue and federal grants for preservation and services to the elderly.

1899. Burnham and Root
Chicago, Burlington and Quincy Railroad, West Iowa Division—Creston Station
116 West Adams (Union County)

Norfolk Old City Hall

Norfolk, Virginia

This Second Renaissance Revival–style structure, built as the U.S. Post Office and Federal Courts Building, was constructed in response to the tremendous growth the port of Norfolk enjoyed at the end of the 19th century. Reassuringly monumental, the building displays such classical features as a banded first floor, projecting three central bays, balcony and shield within the pediment. Its most dramatic feature, however, is the skylighted courtyard. The city hall was designed by the Baltimore architectural firm of James B. N. Wyatt and William G. Nolting, who had a successful practice designing residences, churches and public buildings in the Maryland and Washington, D.C., area. The building served as the city hall from 1938 to 1965, and until 1977 it was used by a city agency. Interior alterations have been carried out five times. The building has been sold to a developer for conversion to office use.

1899–1900. Wyatt and Nolting
U.S. Post Office and Federal Courts Building
235 East Plume Street

110

Newark City Hall

Newark, New Jersey

"In formally accepting and opening so magnificent a public building, I am impressed by its beauty and massiveness, a grandeur which I can compare to no other building in all these Eastern States," said Mayor Henry M. Doremus at the 1906 dedication. "This is our City Hall, of which we are proud because it proves that we are a progressive people." Even allowing for a politician's hyperbole, Doremus's statement reflects much about early 20th-century attitudes toward government and architecture. The years following the turn of the century were characterized by progressivism and municipal government reform, and these lofty ideals were naturally associated with grand, massive, beautiful architecture. Concomitant with the reform movement was the use of architectural competitions, which were considered a less biased, less corrupt way of selecting architects. The Beaux-Arts classicism embodied in Newark's city hall, the product of a design competition, was ideally suited for such structures. The building's outstanding exterior features are its massiveness and three-dimensionality, which contrast with its fine interior features. The depth of the engaged columns, the setback of the windows, the projecting pavilions and the dome give depth and interest to what, in the hands of less skilled designers, would be a massive but bland exterior. The gracefully curving staircase, large rotunda, rich detailing and baroque skylight create the drama of space and movement that is the essence of architecture. John and Wilson Ely were Newark architects whose most important buildings were Baby's Hospital and the New Jersey Memorial Building, as well as Newark City Hall. Frank Grod, of the firm Mowbray and Uffinger, designed an annex and connecting bridge in 1928.

1902–06. John H. and Wilson C. Ely. 1928. Mowbray and Uffinger
920 Broad Street (Essex County)
National Register of Historic Places

University City City Hall
University City, Missouri

Designed with ornate terra–cotta detailing that harmonizes with the detailing of the 1904 St. Louis World's Fair buildings, located a mile away, this structure was built as the headquarters for publishing entrepreneur Edward Gardner Lewis. In addition to his several highly popular magazines for women, Lewis is credited with starting the first mail–order bank and organizing the first convention of the American Women's League. He was also University City's first mayor, and his building served as the city hall until 1911, when a new city hall opened. In 1930 the city government offices moved back into the building and have remained here since. Along with the city gates, the building marks the entrance to University City. The structure's green dome once supported a high-power beacon that was lighted for the World's Fair, and behind the elaborate fifth-floor windows was once a 35-foot-high ballroom. Even so, the building's most interesting spaces are on the lower floors: the dramatic colonnaded, suspended staircase and Lewis's luxuriously decorated offices. The murals on the ceilings of the first and second floors were painted by Ralph Schesley Ott, whose murals also appear in the Missouri State Capitol and St. Louis City Hall. When the building again became University City's city hall, the fifth floor was modified for use as the city council chamber.

1903–04. Herbert C. Chivers
Woman's Magazine Building
6801 Delmar Boulevard (St. Louis County)

Savannah City Hall

Savannah, Georgia

Savannah is known for its 18th-century town plan with its focus on small parks, so it is fitting that its city hall, with its tower, is a highly visible terminus for the parks on Bull Street. The building was intended to have a more lively silhouette. A quadriga (sculptures of chariots and horses) was proposed for the corner of the fifth-floor roof but was not constructed for budgetary reasons; if it had been built, the city hall's domed tower would have related better to the building's lower stories. The design is more successful on the interior, where a four-story rotunda culminates in a colorful, stained-glass dome. Hyman Witcover was a Savannah architect whose work consisted predominantly of residences. The structure is built on the site of the city exchange, a late 18th-century building that housed the municipal government, and overlooks the Savannah River. Most of the building's ceilings have been lowered and several offices subdivided. The exterior, however, is unaltered.

1904–05. Hyman W. Witcover
Bay and Bull Streets (Chatham County)

The District Building

Washington, D.C.

The District Building, which houses Washington's mayor's office and some city offices, is a subdued version of the Beaux-Arts style. It has the typical classical coupled columns, symmetry, five-part composition, exterior sculpture (by De Nesti and Ernest C. Bairstoro) and wide interior staircase. These features, however, are not expressed adequately to create a vigorous, three-dimensional facade, an interesting skyline or dramatic interior spaces. This design was the result of a competition whose guidelines specified "a classic design in the manner of the English Renaissance." The firm of Walter Cope and John and Emlyn Stewardson was one of the leading architectural firms in the Northeast, having designed major buildings at Bryn Mawr, Princeton University and the University of Pennsylvania and the Administration Building at the 1904 Louisiana Purchase Exposition. The building faces Pennsylvania Avenue and occupies a prominent location near the White House. Since the Kennedy Administration, efforts have been made to revitalize Pennsylvania Avenue between the U.S. Capitol and the White House. With new parks and buildings opposite the District Building, its immediate environs are considerably improved. The south side of Pennsylvania Avenue between the Federal Triangle and the District Building, however, is still an unattractive parking lot. Interior spaces have been partitioned and have undergone other alterations.

1904–08. Cope and Stewardson
1350 Pennsylvania Avenue, N.W.

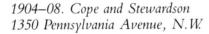

Dayton Municipal Building
Dayton, Ohio

Dayton's municipal building derives its architectural and historical merit from its association with the Young Men's Christian Association. When constructed, it was supposedly the second largest YMCA in the world and the embodiment of architectural fashion with its Georgian Revival detailing—keystones, columns, pedimented lintels and contrasting red brick and white stone. The building's architects—Luther Peters, George Hermann and Clifford C. Brown—were Dayton residents. During Dayton's devastating flood of 1913, the building was the center of relief activities, housing the Red Cross hospital, emergency cafeteria, board of health, state militia and other agencies. When the building was purchased by the city in 1940, it was altered for what was expected to be temporary use as the city hall; however, it has served in that capacity ever since. Although the swimming pool, gymnasium and auditorium have been floored over, the original six-story staircase, mosaic floors and marble panels remain. The building's rear section is apparently original, despite its setback and changes in detailing.

1906–08. The Architect's League, Ltd. (Luther Peters, George Hermann and Clifford C. Brown)
Young Men's Christian Association, Dayton Industries Building
101 West Third Street (Montgomery County)

Little Rock City Hall

Little Rock, Arkansas

As designed and built, Little Rock's city hall was an ambitious building in the period's approved municipal architectural style, Beaux-Arts. The architect, Charles Thompson, was a well-known and prolific Arkansas architect, primarily of public buildings. The city hall has grand staircases on its two major elevations and a high dome on a drum. On the interior, the rotunda has a mosaic tile floor and, above, a brightly colored, leaded-glass skylight, which has been restored. From the rotunda, a wide, divided staircase leads to the upper floors. Since the 1960s, the city has made a number of changes, largely in the name of energy conservation. The interior features have been preserved, but of the original exterior features, only the stairs remain, thus giving the building its current warehouse look. Despite its appearance, it is still being used as the city hall. During Little Rock's rapid growth in the 1950s and 1960s, there was a move to demolish the overcrowded building and erect a larger facility. Instead, some city departments have been moved to other buildings.

1907–08. Charles L. Thompson
500 West Markham Street (Pulaski County)
National Register of Historic Places

Yonkers City Hall

Yonkers, New York

Austrian architect Adolf Loos wrote in 1908: "As ornament is no longer organically linked with our culture, it is also no longer an expression of our culture." Yonkers City Hall, under construction at that time, has a great deal of surface ornament that, 75 years later, seems to bear no relationship to either Yonkers's culture or the building itself. Variously described as "non-academic Beaux-Arts style" and "a free interpretation of neobaroque forms," the building and its decoration seem better suited to early 20th-century Florida, with its Spanish baroque heritage. This building's glory is its siting and interior. Built on Yonkers's highest point, it overlooks the original business district. Also on the site are two other, less monumental municipal buildings—the public library (1903) and the health center (1929). The public library and city hall are the two best-known works of H. Lansing Quick, a Yonkers native. The interior has an ornate, grand rotunda, circled by a sweeping staircase; the council room has a stained-glass skylight and 10 murals by Richard Vincente Adorente and A. E. Fortinger of New York City. In 1959 Princess Beatrix of the Netherlands visited the building to commemorate Yonkers's origins as a Dutch trading post, and in 1976 President Ford signed the Revenue Sharing Act here. The building has had the usual interior alterations, such as addition of partitions.

1907–10. H. Lansing Quick
Washington Park (Westchester County)
National Register of Historic Places

Berkeley Old City Hall
Berkeley, California

John Bakewell and Arthur Brown won the Berkeley City Hall competition with a design that was supposedly inspired by the town hall in Tours, France. It is understandable that they would use a European town hall as their model. Both men were educated at the Ecole des Beaux-Arts in Paris, and Brown, the designer in the firm, had studied under the architect of the Tours town hall. At the Ecole, architects were trained to base their designs on classical architecture. This approach resulted in rather precise borrowing of motifs and plans from acknowledged architectural masterpieces. A local newspaper in 1908 described the building as "monumental architecture," and such details as the unusually robust balcony consoles, prominent cupola and engaged columns with entablatures and urns do have a monumental quality. That same grandeur is evident in the interior, especially in the staircase. Built on the site of the preceding city hall, this building was the first element of the Berkeley civic center complex, which apparently was inspired by the turn-of-the-century City Beautiful movement and which consists of four public buildings around a landscaped green. The City Beautiful movement was also an outgrowth of the Ecole des Beaux-Arts, with its emphasis on formal planning—not only of buildings, but also of the relationships among buildings. The most dramatic demonstration of the great beauty that could be achieved through Beaux-Arts architecture and planning was the 1893 Columbian Exposition in Chicago, with its "Great White Way." Buildings of shared color, size and detailing flanked a great lagoon, creating an architectural ensemble that through photographs has continued to captivate the American mind 80 years after it was disassembled. Bakewell and Brown later designed several major California buildings, including the city halls of San Francisco and Pasadena. The nonpublic interior spaces have been altered several times, and in 1950 the rear wings flanking the outside stair walls were erected. The city government vacated the building in 1977, and since 1980 it has served as the administrative offices for the school district, although the city council and the board of education continue to meet in the building.

1908–09. John Bakewell, Jr., and Arthur Brown, Jr.
2134 Grove Street (Alameda County)

Trenton Municipal Building

Trenton, New Jersey

By the early 20th century, classical architecture had become the preferred style for public buildings, from city halls to the new Senate and House office buildings designed by Carrère and Hastings for the U.S. Congress. This building's marble, symmetrical facades, with two-story columns, bronze gates, banding and elaborate lintels, were designed to impress the viewer with the importance of the institution housed within. But the grandest sight is reserved for those who visit the two-story council chamber. Decorated with a coffered ceiling, elaborate wall frets and capitals, the room has as its focus two Everett Shinn murals depicting steel and pottery manufacturing, two of the city's most important industries. Spencer Roberts was a Philadelphia architect who also designed the Trenton Free Public Library. In the late 1970s, a starkly contemporary annex was built parallel to the city hall. Connected to the older building by a three-story hyphen, the annex shares the facade material, height and general shape of the original building. The annex was designed by John Clark, AIA, Fred Travisano, AIA, and Richard Bartels, AIA, in association with Franklyn Spiezle, AIA.

1908–10. Spencer Roberts
Trenton City Hall and City Hall Annex
319 East State Street (Mercer County)
National Register of Historic Places

Indianapolis City Hall
Indianapolis, Indiana

As the Indianapolis city government had always used leased space for its offices, presumably Mayor Charles A. Bookwalter's proposal in 1907 to erect a city hall and auditorium on the city market site would have been favorably received. Instead, his plans were blocked by a lawsuit brought by two butchers from the market. The next year the mayor held a design competition for a more modest proposal on a different site, having dropped the idea of an auditorium. Another controversy arose when the commission was awarded to Rubush and Hunter, one of Indiana's leading architectural firms, which had previously been retained by the mayor to draw plans for the first proposal. The losing architects, supported by a newspaper owned by a political opponent of Bookwalter, complained that Rubush and Hunter's building estimates were too low and that the firm should not have won the competition. In turn, a competing newspaper came to the defense of the mayor. Despite the political and architectural machinations, Indianapolis succeeded in getting a properly imposing Beaux-Arts city hall, with the typical two-story engaged columns, flanked by slightly projecting pavilions. The most architecturally exciting features are on the interior: a four-story atrium crowned with a stained-glass skylight, a grand staircase and classically inspired murals, columns and other detailing. In 1962 the city moved its offices into a joint city-county building and announced its intention to sell the building. The state leased the building the next year, and from 1964 to 1966 the architecture-engineering firm of James Associates adapted the building for use as the state musuem. At that time, the window openings were sealed with limestone, ceilings lowered and offices combined into larger gallery spaces. The museum saved the eagles from D. H. Burnham and Company's Traction Terminal Building in Indianapolis, now demolished, and mounted them in front of the building on bases that originally supported three-story-high bronze flagpoles. In 1973 the state purchased the building for continued use as the Indiana State Museum and the offices of the Indiana Department of Natural Resources.

1909–10. Rubush and Hunter
Indiana State Museum
202 North Alabama Street (Marion County)

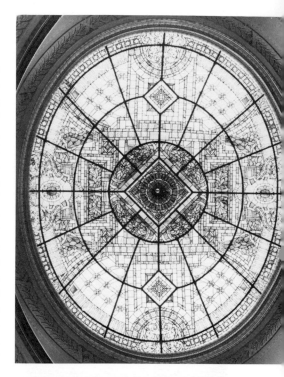

Sacramento City Hall

Sacramento, California

Rudolph Herold was a San Francisco native who spent three years studying and practicing architecture in Europe. When he returned in 1898, he moved to Sacramento, where he designed several public buildings, including hospitals, schools and courthouses. His designs, as seen in Sacramento's city hall, reflect his exposure to Beaux-Arts architecture and planning. The city hall has the familiar Beaux-Arts preference for classical detailing, such as the engaged columns, urns and entablature. With its tall, central clock tower, the building is the focus not only of its landscaped park but also of the larger surrounding area. This formal landscape planning, organized around a focal point, is a characteristic of Beaux-Arts planning. In the 1930s two annexes were built, one of them funded by the WPA. The interiors have been remodeled, and little original detail can be found in such spaces as the two-story council chamber. The Sacramento City Hall remains the center of city government.

1909–11. Rudolph Herold
915 I Street (Sacramento County)

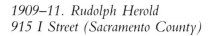

Chicago City Hall
Chicago, Illinois

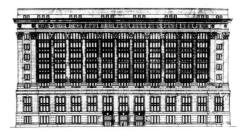

Daniel H. Burnham, the Chicago architect and urban planner prominent at the turn of the century, said, "Make no little plans." This building, designed by another of Chicago's prolific and nationally influential architectural firms, lives up to that credo, for the building's outstanding quality is its monumentality. The architect's original rendering shows this building dwarfing its slightly older commercial neighbors; now, 70 years later, the structure is surrounded by buildings all taller than it—including the Richard J. Daley Civic Center, an immense skyscraper—but it is not overwhelmed. Its massive colonnade of Corinthian columns on a three-story base successfully counters its taller but less substantial neighbors. This building, Chicago's seventh city hall and the third joint city-county facility, is located on the site that since 1853, except for one brief period, has been occupied by a city hall or county building. Cook County and the city of Chicago held a design competition for the half of the building each was to occupy. Holabird and Roche, best known for pioneering skyscraper designs, won both competitions, but the county held its competition earlier and began construction two years before the city did. The city's progress was delayed while it awaited a state decree to raise Chicago's limit of bond indebtedness. Despite the hiatus, the city-county building is an integrated structure with no obvious evidence of any difference between the two occupants or periods of construction. Exterior alterations appear limited to the removal of the cornice in the 1940s, but the interior underwent substantial alterations from 1967 to 1972. In the 1950s a fire in the two-story council chamber destroyed its murals, and the room was remodeled with modern decoration.

1909–11. Holabird and Roche
Public square bounded by LaSalle, Washington, Clark and Randolph Streets (Cook County)

Lynchburg Old City Hall
Lynchburg, Virginia

Lynchburg's old city hall reflects the characteristics of the Second Renaissance Revival style—symmetry, a rusticated first floor with round-arched openings, a bracketed, overhanging cornice and shouldered window architraves—and has the quiet dignity common to federal and public buildings of the late 19th and early 20th centuries. Such buildings lack the architectural power of their predecessors, such as the Richardsonian Romanesque city halls, but their detailing and choice of materials save them from being ordinary. James Taylor, as supervising architect of the U.S. Treasury Department from 1897 to 1912, was responsible for many federal buildings executed in various popular architectural styles. Built as a post office and courthouse to replace an 1885 Romanesque Revival–style post office that stood on the site, this structure served as the city hall from 1933 to 1982. To the right of the building are Monument Terrace, which is a 1920s World War I memorial, and an 1855 courthouse with a monumental staircase; these buildings provide a Renaissance and baroque urban setting, appropriate for this city hall. Despite several interior alterations during the 1960s and 1970s, the WPA mural depicting a planter transporting tobacco to market still remains in the lobby. The building now serves as an annex to the present city hall, located directly across the street.

1909–12. James Knox Taylor
City Hall Annex
901 Church Street

Springfield City Hall

Springfield, Massachusetts

When former President William Howard Taft dedicated the Springfield City Hall, he probably had no notion of what a telling architectural statement the three-structure complex made. In their competition-winning design, the architects, Livingston Pell and Harvey Corbett, designed a campanile, loosely based on the medieval-Renaissance campanile in Venice's Piazza San Marco, flanked by two classical revival temples, one housing the city hall and one housing the city auditorium. Such architectural eclecticism, rare in any period, was most successfully done by early 20th-century architects and, on a more modest scale, by present-day postmodernists. Despite his early eclecticism, Corbett, who was educated at the Ecole des Beaux-Arts, is probably best known for his work on Rockefeller Center and the Chicago World's Fair of 1933, both modernistic architectural designs. Pell was an architect trained at Columbia University and in Europe who collaborated with Corbett in this competition and in one for the Maryland Institute of Design in Baltimore. The main doors of the campanile, auditorium and city hall each consist of 16 bronze panels designed by Gail Sherman Corbett, the architect's wife. The interior of the building has a grand staircase, classically decorated marble corridors and public rooms faced in mahogany. In 1922 the first floor of the building's courtyard was enclosed to provide additional office space.

1909–13. F. Livingston Pell and Harvey Wiley Corbett
Campanile, Municipal Auditorium, Springfield Municipal Group
36 Court Street (Hampden County)

Pittsfield City Hall

Pittsfield, Massachusetts

In the 1901 annual report of the supervising architect of the U.S. Treasury Department, James Knox Taylor wrote, "The Department, after mature consideration of the subject, finally decided to adopt the classic style of architecture for all buildings as far as it was practicable to do so, and it is believed that this style is best suited for government buildings." Hardly the largest or best example of neoclassical federal architecture, this structure, originally built as Pittsfield's post office, is typical of Taylor's designs in the early 20th century. Taylor, who was Treasury supervising architect from 1897 to 1912, designed several major post offices, the one in San Francisco (1905) being the best known. This small building in western Massachusetts demonstrates the desire of the federal government to establish a presence, through stylistically current architecture, throughout the country. As a highly competent rendering of Beaux-Arts architecture, the building could only improve the architectural quality of downtown Pittsfield. That the building's quality endures is reflected in its continued use even after the post office moved to other facilities. The building was also Pittsfield's first with a revolving door. In the 1930s an addition was made in the rear, and in 1967 the building was renovated by architect John H. Fisher for use as the city hall. As part of the conversion, the interior was renovated and some original mahogany painted.

1910. James Knox Taylor
U.S. Post Office
66 Allen Street (Berkshire County)
National Register of Historic Places

Des Moines City Hall

Des Moines, Iowa

This building's commonplace Beaux-Arts facade belies its historical and symbolic importance. On June 7, 1907, the people of Des Moines voted to institute a new form of government and to erect a new city hall. The new commission type of city management was based on the progressive concept of open government run by commissioners, drawn from the city's elite, rather than backroom rule by ward bosses. The open government ideal was architecturally expressed by the building's interior: In the large main room, or counting room, city employees would carry out their responsibilities in the open, under the careful strutiny of the citizenry. The room's barrel-vaulted, skylighted ceiling has handsomely decorated panels. The building, situated on the east side of the Des Moines River, was an important element in a plan to improve the riverfront area and create an architecturally appropriate approach to the state capitol. This plan, which reflected the principles of the then-popular City Beautiful movement, was never implemented. The architects associated with designing the city hall were the state's most distinguished. Henry Liebbe was the first state architect, Harry Rawson was the first registered architect in Iowa, and Frank Wetherell was a leader in the local City Beautiful movement. The others were prolific Iowa architects.

1910–11. Liebbe, Nourse and Rasmussen; Hallett and Rawson; Wetherell and Gage; Proudfoot and Bird
Municipal Building
East First and Locust Streets (Polk County)
National Register of Historic Places

Oakland City Hall
Oakland, California

Oakland has long been in San Francisco's shadow; the latter's city hall is nationally recognized, while Oakland's is probably little known outside the Bay Area. Even the city's pride in having President William Howard Taft attend the 1911 cornerstone ceremony for its new city hall must have been diminished somewhat when he then traveled across the bay to attend a similar ceremony for San Francisco's Pan-Pacific International Exposition. Despite the design competition held for the city hall and the winning architect's innovative design, the prophecy of Oakland mayor's would not be fulfilled: "This type of building, being out of the original and conventional style, will attract notice everywhere, and will put Oakland in front ranks of modern cities in the magnificence and attractiveness of its chief public building." John Galen Howard, FAIA, director of the University of California's School of Architecture, was the adviser to the competition, which paid several nationally prominent architects—among them, McKim, Mead and White, Peabody and Stearns, and Cass Gilbert—$1,000 each to participate. The first-prize winner, Palmer and Hornbostel, received $5,000. In 1904 the firm had won a competition for the Carnegie Institute of Technology, whose School of Architecture was founded and directed by Henry Hornbostel; Palmer and Hornbostel also won the city hall competitions for Pittsburgh (1915–17) and Wilmington, Del. (1914–17). The building is an office skyscraper placed on a wider base and overlaid with vaguely classical details (e.g., columns) and Federal-style details (e.g., the cupola and eagles), while those of the balustrades seem inspired by Viollet-le-Duc. The detailing of the grapevine stringcourses and grand marble staircase is heavy. In addition to the ceremonial public rooms, such as the multistory vestibule, rotunda and council chamber, the lower stories housed the fire department and firemen's dormitories, police department and courts. Most floors in the tower were conventional municipal offices, but the 12th, 13th and 14th housed the city prison and emergency hospital. The structure, which occupies an entire city block, was built on a site adjacent to the preceding city hall.

1911–14. Palmer and Hornbostel
14th and Washington Streets (Alameda County)

Grand Forks City Hall

Grand Forks, North Dakota

This city hall is one of four extant early 20th-century neoclassical buildings erected by the city and federal governments in Grand Forks. This building, along with a high school and post office–courthouse, form an architectural ensemble that, according to a local historian, reflects "the city's regional importance to a vast agricultural hinterland in the Red River Valley at the turn of the century." In style and color, the building is consistent with late, restrained classicism: It features stone quoins, roof balustrades and limited use of columns and is constructed of yellow brick. The existence of this building in a community as small and remote as Grand Forks suggests how widespread the neoclassical style was. John Ross was a Grand Forks architect who designed buildings in eastern North Dakota and northern Minnesota between the 1890s and 1940. The major alteration has been the removal of the original doors and windows.

1911. John W. Ross
404 Second Avenue North (Grand Forks County)

Cleveland City Hall
Cleveland, Ohio

This structure cannot be fully appreciated when viewed in isolation; it should be examined as a critical element in the 1903 mall (or group) plan by Daniel H. Burnham, Arnold Brunner and John M. Carrère. This plan, typical of those of the turn-of-the-century City Beautiful movement, derives from Chicago's 1893 World's Columbian Exposition, whose planning Burnham directed. Sharing the fair's symmetrical layout and classical architecture, the Cleveland mall plan, as built, groups major public buildings around three sides of a green, with the fourth side open to Lake Erie. The city hall forms one of the anchors of the mall, delineating the northeast corner of the complex, which also includes the Federal Reserve Bank, U.S. Post Office and Court House, Cuyahoga County Court House, Board of Education Building, Public Auditorium and Music Hall and Cleveland Public Library. The projected union depot, which would have filled the fourth side of the mall, was never built. The architect, J. Milton Dyer, was educated at the Ecole des Beaux-Arts and in Cleveland. Although the majority of his projects were in Cleveland, he also designed the U.S. Sub-Treasury Building in San Francisco. The city hall's facades are designed in a restrained neoclassical style, which is counterbalanced by the striking interior spaces and finishes. Running transversely through the building is the skylighted, coffered, barrel-vaulted, multistory Great Hall, 100 feet long and 55 feet wide. The hall's elaborate light stands, railings, murals and ceiling details are, however, surpassed by the two-story council chamber and the mayor's office suite, both of which have a wealth of original, ornate furnishings, carved woodwork and wall and ceiling decorations. The council chamber was renovated in 1951; at that time Ivor Johns's mural, originally in Cleveland's old Central National Bank Building, was installed. In 1972–73 the mayor's rooms were renovated and the 1916 tapestries cleaned. The underground parking garage to the rear of the building was constructed in 1975.

1912–14. J. Milton Dyer
601 Lakeside Avenue (Cuyahoga County)
National Register of Historic Places

North Little Rock City Hall

North Little Rock, Arkansas

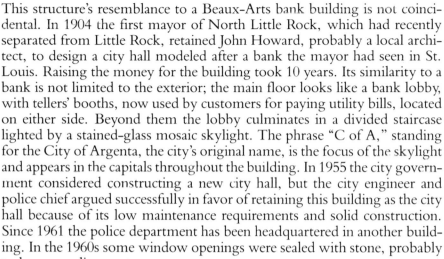

This structure's resemblance to a Beaux-Arts bank building is not coincidental. In 1904 the first mayor of North Little Rock, which had recently separated from Little Rock, retained John Howard, probably a local architect, to design a city hall modeled after a bank the mayor had seen in St. Louis. Raising the money for the building took 10 years. Its similarity to a bank is not limited to the exterior; the main floor looks like a bank lobby, with tellers' booths, now used by customers for paying utility bills, located on either side. Beyond them the lobby culminates in a divided staircase lighted by a stained-glass mosaic skylight. The phrase "C of A," standing for the City of Argenta, the city's original name, is the focus of the skylight and appears in the capitals throughout the building. In 1955 the city government considered constructing a new city hall, but the city engineer and police chief argued successfully in favor of retaining this building as the city hall because of its low maintenance requirements and solid construction. Since 1961 the police department has been headquartered in another building. In the 1960s some window openings were sealed with stone, probably to lower cooling costs.

1914. John L. Howard
Third and Main Streets (Pulaski County)

San Francisco City Hall

San Francisco, California

San Francisco's city hall has been described as the focal point of the best architectural ensemble in America. Included in this ensemble are the building's immediate northern neighbors—the War Veterans Memorial Building and War Memorial Opera House (both 1932, Arthur Brown and G. Albert Lansburgh)—with Thomas Church's landscaped courtyard between them. The south facade faces a formally landscaped city block; it is flanked on the east by the state office building (1926, Walter Bliss and William Faville) and on the east by the civic auditorium (1913, John Galen Howard, Fred Mayer and John Reid, Jr.). Howard, Mayer and Reid were retained as the commissioners for the design competition for this city hall. This Beaux-Arts masterpiece, with its graceful massing, domed rotunda, grand staircase and detailing, was designed as the focus of a plan incorporating the principles of the City Beautiful movement. In the Beaux-Arts tradition, Arthur Brown drew on European predecessors for the design of the dome, specifically those of St. Peter's, Les Invalides, the Val de Grace and St. Paul's. The exterior and interior sculpture is by Henri Crenier. This city hall is an architectural statement of the grandeur of the city-state and, in fact, looks more like a state capitol than a city hall. Seldom are architecture and planning so well integrated, where neither element is diminished to enhance the other; San Francisco City Hall is a strong building within as strong a landscape.

1913–15. John Bakewell, Jr., and Arthur Brown, Jr.
Civic Center (San Francisco County)

Wilmington Public Building

Wilmington, Delaware

The design for this Beaux-Arts building, with its symmetry and classical columns and pilasters, was the winner of a design competition. The competition guidelines did not prescribe a specific style but did proscribe towers and domes, which, in late 19th- and early 20th-century American architecture, were no longer fashionable. The competition was restricted to 11 firms, three of which were invited to participate. In keeping with early 20th-century progressivism and concern with honest government, a professor of architecture, rather than politicians, judged the competition submissions. At the urging of John J. Raskob, secretary of the DuPont Company, the city and county undertook a joint building and erected it facing Rodney Square. Both the city of Wilmington and New Castle County had outgrown their current facilities. Since 1905 Pierre S. DuPont, influenced by the City Beautiful movement, had been leading efforts to make that area the city's civic center, and his efforts were eventually successful: Rodney Square is bounded by the Wilmington Institute Free Library, U.S. Post Office and the Hotel DuPont, in addition to the city hall, and these structures form an architecturally harmonious grouping. In 1960 the city hall's left wing was enlarged by Whiteside, Moeckel and Carbonell, a local firm. The large vaulted central corridor was converted into a courtroom in 1974, and a rear wing was enlarged for the police department in 1980. The state acquired the building in the same year and has undertaken substantial alterations under the direction of Diamond McCune, architects and engineers. The city-county building, however, continues to house some city departments and courtrooms.

1914–17. Palmer, Hornbostel and Jones
City-County Building
1000 King Street (New Castle County)

Tampa City Hall

Tampa, Florida

The architectural drama created by Tampa's city hall and its stylistically matching three-story police station and jail (since demolished) has been lost as concrete and reflective-glass skyscrapers have risen around the building. What today looks like a squat, compressed building originally had a sense of majestic height, reinforced by its three setbacks. With its relatively large expanse of glass, neoclassical columns, sculpted heads, other unusual surface decoration and the mansard-roof clock tower, Tampa's city hall demonstrates that municipal buildings do not have to be either staid, inflexible classical mausoleums or commonplace commercial structures. Leo Elliott was a Tampa architect with one of the largest practices in the South specializing in educational and commercial buildings. Rowe Holmes Associates, Architects, has restored the building for continued use as office space and council chambers. The mayor's office is located in an adjacent 1978 municipal building.

1915. M. Leo Elliott
315 East Kennedy Boulevard (Hillsborough County)
National Register of Historic Places

Roanoke Municipal Building and Courthouse

Roanoke, Virginia

As with other public buildings of the early 20th century, the style used here is classically inspired. What distinguishes this building from other municipal and public buildings is the large amount of glass used. The building combines the monumentality of neoclassical architecture—a wide exterior staircase, three-story entrance pavilion and two-story columns and pilasters—with the efficiency of factory architecture—e.g., large areas of glass providing abundant natural lighting. E. F. Frye was a Roanoke architect, while Chesterman returned to Lynchburg after working on this and three other projects. Originally, police offices, including the court, detention area and dorms, were housed on the first floor; administrative offices, including the mayor's offices, were located on the second; the council chamber, ornate, oak-finished courtrooms and support facilities were on the third floor; and the jail was on the fourth and fifth floors. With the completion in 1970 of an attached annex by Hayes, Seay, Mattern and Mattern, the administrative offices moved to the annex and the police offices moved to another building, leaving the original municipal buildings solely for court use. With the completion of a new courthouse, it is expected that the old municipal building will be renovated and used again by city agencies.

1915–16. Frye and Chesterman
216 Campbell Avenue, S.W.

Cheyenne City and County Building

Cheyenne, Wyoming

In November 1914 the city of Cheyenne and Laramie County agreed to construct a joint building to reduce their maintenance costs. The city and county building, built on the site of the county courthouse, demonstrates the adaptability of the neoclassical style to smaller cities. Although the neoclassical public buildings of larger cities are usually faced in stone and, hence, more impressive, Cheyenne's is predominantly red brick, which provides a pleasing contrast to the light masonry of the base, columns, name panel and entablature. Because a clock tower would be inappropriate for a neoclassical building, there is a simple clock in the parapet of one of the short sides of the building. The building's only elaborate spaces are the court-rooms. The architect, William Dubois, designed numerous institutional buildings and residences in Cheyenne and was also a member of the Wyoming legislature. In 1957 an annex was erected. The building is occupied entirely by the county government, as the city offices have been relocated.

1917–19. William R. Dubois
County Courthouse
19th Street and Carey Avenue (Laramie County)
National Register of Historic Places

Pittsburgh City-County Building

Pittsburgh, Pennsylvania

Pittsburgh's city-county building has the disadvantage of being adjacent to H. H. Richardson's Allegheny County Courthouse and Jail (1888), perhaps the architect's most praised work. The differences between the buildings reflect not only the difference between architectural genius and considerable competence but also, more fundamental, the change in times and clients' requirements. Between 1900 and 1920, the desired statement in public architecture was not one of manifest destiny or robustness but one of the grandeur and dignity of the government unit responsible for erecting the building. Henry Hornbostel, who won this commission through an architectural competition supervised by Cass Gilbert, used the common motifs of classical columns and pilasters to evoke the dignity of city and county governments, but he went even further. He added grandeur with the multistory entrance arcade on Grant Street, which opens onto the interior grand gallery extending the length of the building. The barrel-vaulted, 47-foot-high gallery is lined by raised, multistory bronze columns separating it from the light wells on either side. The original door and ceiling treatments of the mayor's office have Georgian Revival moldings. By contrast, the two-story council chamber is not decorated in any specific historical style. Above these rooms are the floors used by the courts. The top floor originally housed the city's now antiquated fire-alarm system; that floor has been converted to a municipal cable television studio. Lacking the three-dimensional quality of the Allegheny County Courthouse but not impaired by an excess of detailing, the city-county building makes a strong architectural statement, on both the exterior and interior. The little detailing that exists—in the cornice and above the entrances—effectively relieves the flat wall surfaces.

1915–17. Palmer, Hornbostel and Jones; Edward B. Lee
414 Grant Street (Allegheny County)

Littleton Town Hall

Littleton, Colorado

This Gothic-Moorish town hall, with fire station and offices on the first floor and auditorium on the second, owes much to private generosity. The architect not only donated the iron lamps, which he had commissioned, but also convinced the Denver Terra Cotta Company to sell the terra cotta for the facade to the city at cost and to install it for free. Jules Benedict was a major Colorado architect and Littleton resident who was known for his period architecture and fine attention to detail. The building's three arcaded entrances have been enclosed with stucco and glass, and both floors have been partitioned. In 1977 the city moved its offices to a new city hall and leased this building to the Littleton Center for Cultural Arts, which is restoring the facade and adapting the interior for performances and related uses.

1920. Jules Jacques Benoit Benedict
Littleton Center for Cultural Arts
2450 West Main Street (Arapahoe County)
National Register of Historic Places

Texarkana Municipal Building

Texarkana, Texas

Texarkana's city hall appears to be a modest exercise in neoclassical architecture when compared with other, larger public buildings of the period, but it is still an ambitious building. The main facade has a rusticated first floor with three central, segmentally arched openings; above these are three-story fluted, Ionic columns set in antis. The flanking bays are organized into three-story units capped with lintels, and the building is crowned with an entablature and ornamented parapet. The building's most impressive interior feature is the substantial staircase that splits at the first landing. The structure also houses the Sixth District Court of Civil Appeals and the nation's first federal credit union. The credit union was located in Texarkana because the senator responsible for the Federal Credit Union Act was from Texarkana. D. H. Page and Brother were Austin architects, while Witt, Seibert and Halsey was a Texarkana firm.

1924–25. C. H. Page and Brother; Witt, Seibert and Halsey
Texas Boulevard and Third Street (Bowie County)

St. Joseph City Hall

St. Joseph, Missouri

In the 1920s, when the city of St. Joseph decided to build a city hall and civic center, it looked to Europe for inspiration. Jacques Greber, an internationally known city planner and landscape architect from Paris, was retained to draw up a Beaux-Arts landscape plan with the city hall as one focus and a war memorial as the second. The city hall itself, designed by the prominent St. Joseph architects Edmund Jacques Eckel and Will S. Aldrich, is in the Renaissance Revival style. According to the July 2, 1927, issue of the St. Joseph *News-Press*, "Permanency and art were the thoughts of the architects when they designed the new building. They wanted to give St. Joseph a building of a style which would survive half a century, three quarters or even 100 years, if the people found this desirable—a building which would appeal to the future as well as the present." The entrance lobby and the mayor's office are the building's most attractive interior features. The split-level entrance lobby is a highly formal space, with a gilded, coffered ceiling and polished stone columns, pilasters and floor. The mayor's office has elegant wood floors and walls and a patterned ceiling suggestive of baroque churches. A two-block landscaped park was created behind the city hall, with a symmetrically placed fountain and a sculpture commemorating the World War I dead.

1924–27. Eckel and Aldrich
11th Street and Frederick Avenue (Buchanan County)

142

Pasadena City Hall

Pasadena, California

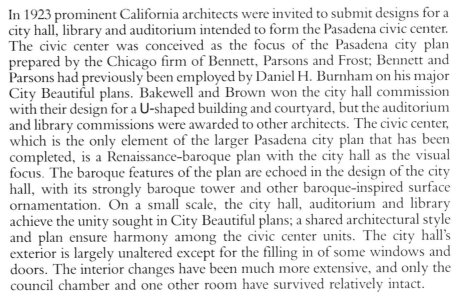

In 1923 prominent California architects were invited to submit designs for a city hall, library and auditorium intended to form the Pasadena civic center. The civic center was conceived as the focus of the Pasadena city plan prepared by the Chicago firm of Bennett, Parsons and Frost; Bennett and Parsons had previously been employed by Daniel H. Burnham on his major City Beautiful plans. Bakewell and Brown won the city hall commission with their design for a U-shaped building and courtyard, but the auditorium and library commissions were awarded to other architects. The civic center, which is the only element of the larger Pasadena city plan that has been completed, is a Renaissance-baroque plan with the city hall as the visual focus. The baroque features of the plan are echoed in the design of the city hall, with its strongly baroque tower and other baroque-inspired surface ornamentation. On a small scale, the city hall, auditorium and library achieve the unity sought in City Beautiful plans; a shared architectural style and plan ensure harmony among the civic center units. The city hall's exterior is largely unaltered except for the filling in of some windows and doors. The interior changes have been much more extensive, and only the council chamber and one other room have survived relatively intact.

1926–27. John Bakewell, Jr., and Arthur Brown, Jr.
100 North Garfield Avenue (Los Angeles County)

Los Angeles City Hall
Los Angeles, California

Before Los Angeles could build its 452-foot-high city hall, the electorate had to approve an exception to the city's zoning law, which limited buildings to 150 feet or 12 stories. The city's first monumental structure, the city hall reflected the citizens' pride in their city. Although the building has a stepped-back roof and Egyptian, Greek and Roman details, the dedication booklet asserted that the building's architectural style was "modern architecture" and that "no attempt was made to follow the lines of any past or present master builder." The structure has a bilaterally symmetrical first-floor plan with an exuberantly baroque rotunda in the center. Equally ornate are some of the other public rooms, such as the council chamber and public works chamber. John Austin, Albert Martin and John Parkinson, who collaborated on this commission, also worked together on the Los Angeles Terminal Buildings, a group of reinforced concrete structures built in the early 1930s. The sculptors for the city hall were Casper Gruenfeld, Carlo Gerrone and Henry Lion; the murals were painted by Herman Sachs and Antony Heinsbergen. The city hall is the terminus of the civic center mall, an undistinguished civic center plan reflecting the principles of the City Beautiful movement. The only major exterior alteration to the building is a 1971 pedestrian bridge connecting the building to its annex. The major interior public spaces are intact, although the offices have been changed.

1926–28. John C. Austin, Albert C. Martin and John Parkinson
200 North Spring Street (Los Angeles County)

Gary City Hall

Gary, Indiana

In several major American cities, the impetus to undertake large-scale city planning, in keeping with the City Beautiful movement, came not from the government but from leaders of commerce and industry. Gary is a case in point: In 1924 the Gary Commerce Club proposed a Gateway Plan, consisting of a park, courthouse and city hall, that would provide an attractive entrance to the city. The club retained Philip Maher to draft the plan, and he was subsequently selected as the architect for the municipal building as well. Although he had worked three years for his father, George W. Maher, best known for his Wrightian buildings, Philip Maher designed a neoclassical city hall, combining a low Roman dome with Doric columns. The result is a formidable structure that resembles works by Charles Bulfinch in Boston 100 years earlier, such as Massachusetts General Hospital. This heavy-handed attempt at grandeur is repeated on the interior, where multistory windows light the divided staircase. The ceilings of the entrance lobby and second floor are coffered and have large chandeliers. In addition to municipal offices, the building originally contained a citywide fire-alarm system, the police department and a temporary jail. Originally, both main elevations of the building faced landscaped parks, but one has since been paved for use as a parking lot.

1927–28. Philip Brooks Maher
Municipal Building
401 Broadway (Lake County)
National Register of Historic Places

Coral Gables City Hall

Coral Gables, Florida

By the age of 35, George Edgar Merrick, a fruit and vegetable farmer, had 1,600 acres, $500,000 in cash and a city plan and had started selling the first lots in his dream city of Coral Gables. He envisioned a completely planned city of Spanish-style buildings, with loggias, tile roofs and tinted stucco facing. The city hall's distinctive appearance comes from its baroque surface ornamentation and colonnaded semicircular elevation. The reason for using this shape, which is more common to churches than city halls, is unknown. The inspiration for the tower is attributed to that of the city hall of Seville, and the building's major interior staircase may be based on one in Cordova. The mural along the staircase was done in 1957 by John St. John, who also restored Denman Fink's mural in the bell tower ceiling depicting the four seasons. Fink was the art director for Coral Gables, while Phineas Paist was the city's supervising architect and coordinator of color for Coral Gables. Paist was also the associate architect on the Bellevue Stratford Hotel in Philadelphia and the Willard Hotel in Washington, D.C. He and Harold Stewart had formed an architectural firm in 1926, and Stewart was listed as consulting architect on this design project. The building's curved elevation faces Coral Gables's shopping boulevard, while the other main facade overlooks a rose garden. Although the office spaces have been altered considerably since the mid-1950s, the exterior is virtually unchanged.

1927–28. Phineas E. Paist; Denman Fink and Harold Stewart
405 Biltmore Way (Dade County)
National Register of Historic Places

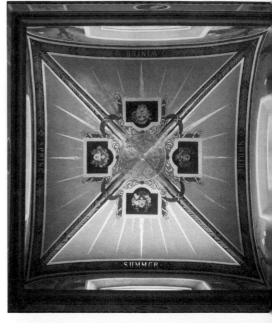

Duluth City Hall

Duluth, Minnesota

By the late 1920s, classically inspired architecture seemed to have run out of inspiration. Buildings such as Duluth's city hall have the expected first-floor rustication, multistory pilasters and dentilled cornice, but each feature lacks depth and power. What passion and effort the designer could summon is reserved for details such as the keystones, the lion-head spandrels and the hall of mayors. The latter, at least, is a properly formal space with much marble and detailing and coffered ceilings. The building's design was chosen by means of an architectural competition restricted to Duluth architects. The winner, Thomas Shefchik, had been educated at the University of Pennsylvania and Ecole des Beaux-Arts and had been in practice only since 1922. This structure, along with a federal building (1930), flanks Daniel H. Burnham's earlier and bolder St. Louis County Courthouse, and it was the county that retained Burnham to plan the three-building civic center. Although Burnham's county courthouse was completed in 1911, it was 17 years before the city hall was built on the site recommended by Burnham. The delay was caused by public controversy over the site selection, cost of the proposed city hall and selection of the architect. As late as 1925, the city government was torn between Burnham's recommended site and one proposed by a city council member. And in late 1925, the newspapers were criticizing the projected cost of the city hall, publishing editorials in favor of a less ornamental, less costly structure. Finally, in November 1925, the city council voided its contract with German and Jenssen to design the city hall and announced it would hold a design competition for the commission, to be judged by three architects from outside Duluth. Why the council cancelled the contract is unknown, but the action was upheld by a district court. The civic center faces Cass Gilbert's Soldiers and Sailors Monument.

1927–28. Thomas J. Shefchik, AIA
411 West First Street (St. Louis County)
National Register of Historic Places

Lexington Town Office Building
Lexington, Massachusetts

In New England municipalities such as Lexington, Revolutionary War associations are so strong that Georgian Revival architecture never goes out of style. In 1927–28 the town's office building, designed by the Boston firm of Kilham, Hopkins, Greeley and Brown, was constructed in that style, and in 1970–71, when the building was enlarged to nearly twice its original size, that style was again used. In fact, the town retained Perry, Dean and Stewart for the enlargement because of that firm's involvement in the restoration of Colonial Williamsburg. A local family, the Careys, donated the land for the town office and adjacent municipal auditorium. It also paid for the construction of the auditorium, which was designed by the same architect and built at the same time. The auditorium and town offices are in separate buildings because the Carey will specified that the bequest not be used to construct administrative offices. But the buildings are in the same style and are sited to form a three-building unit. The Isaac Harris Carey Auditorium is flanked by the smaller town office building and another town building. In 1970–71, the time of the enlargement of the town office building, the interior of the original structure was substantially renovated.

1927–28. Kilham, Hopkins, Greeley and Brown
1625 Massachusetts Avenue (Middlesex County)

Phoenix County-City Administration Building
Phoenix, Arizona

In most joint city-county buildings, both city and county get equal billing in terms of space and architectural expression. This is not the case with Phoenix's county-city building. The major entrance, on a major street, is the county entrance, while the city entrance is on a secondary wing of the building. In fact, the county's architect, Edward Neild, from Shrevesport, La., designed the county courthouse portion and the entire exterior, including the city hall exterior, while the city's architects, the Phoenix firm of Lesher and Mahoney, were left only the city hall interior and the exterior entrance to the city hall wing. That the architectural style was intended to evoke native American architecture rather than the more usual European or Spanish colonial architecture is apparent from the dedication booklet: "The exterior ornamentation suggests immediately to the observers the handiwork of early Americans. This conception is revealed in plastic art and cast bronze throughout the building. To some extent the old world was drawn upon to provide a marble of proper hue and color that would be a link to connect the early life with our present civilization." Today, more than 50 years after completion, little of the building's ornamentation seems native American; the exterior's stonework and the interior's ceiling beams seem to be equally Art Deco in style. Most city and county functions are now housed in newer adjacent facilities, the jail has been closed, and the building's primary user is the courts.

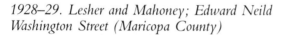

1928–29. Lesher and Mahoney; Edward Neild
Washington Street (Maricopa County)

Atlanta City Hall

Atlanta, Georgia

Atlanta's city hall fits the genre of Gothic skyscraper, the best-known examples being Cass Gilbert's Woolworth Building (1911–13), New York City, and Hood and Howell's Chicago Tribune Tower (1925). In addition to its unusual Gothic detailing, the building is Atlanta's only 1920s setback building. In 1916 New York City had passed a zoning law requiring buildings to occupy less area as they reached certain heights, so as not to block sunlight and fresh air. This law inspired the concept of the setback building, in which higher sections are progressively recessed, the best-known example being the Empire State Building (1929–31, Shreve, Lamb and Harmon). Other cities followed suit, and most of these zoning laws remained in effect until the 1960s. In Atlanta, plans for other setback buildings were scrapped with the onset of the Depression. The concrete structure is faced in cream-colored terra cotta with decorations in olive green. The luxurious lobby is faced in a variety of marble and has bronze fixtures. The city hall was built on a site overlooking Fulton County Court House; the state capitol, in turn, overlooked the courthouse. The building's exterior is unaltered. The most serious interior alteration is the application of accoustical blocks over the wall and ceiling paneling in the council chamber.

1928–30. G. Lloyd Preacher
68 Mitchell Street, S.W. (Fulton County)

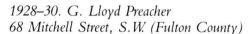

Denver City and County Building
Denver, Colorado

The conservatism of Denver's city-county building should not be attributed to its having been designed by a committee. The building's placement and style date to the Columbian Exposition of 1893 and to the Beaux-Arts concepts of architecture and urban planning, which Denver's mayor, Robert Walton Speer, thought appropriate for an up-and-coming city. In 1906 the city retained Charles Mulford Robinson to design a city plan. His plan called for the city to acquire the land west of the late 19th-century state capitol, designed by Elijah E. Myers, and to build a civic center on the site; the plan was never implemented. In 1916 E. H. Bennett, a city planner who had worked for Daniel Burnham, was retained by the city to prepare another civic center plan. He drew on the proposals of Robinson and sculptor Frederick MacMonnies and designed a plan that incorporated the state capitol as the eastern terminus of a landscaped mall, with the projected city hall as the western terminus. In 1924 a collaboration of Denver's licensed architects was formed to design the city hall. The resulting building is a neoclassical building with a Georgian Revival–style portico and cupola. The most unusual and most important feature of the building is its curved facade, which embraces the formal landscaping, several sculptures and the Board of Water Commissioners Building (built in 1910 as the Denver Public Library), sited between the two end buildings. In addition to the Pioneer Monument, designed by MacMonnies in 1907, 12 memorials, ranging from statues to a colonnade, have been constructed on the mall. The interior of the building has formal, classically decorated spaces; several rooms are faced in marble.

1929–32. Allied Architects Association of Denver
Civic Center (Denver County)

155

Buffalo City Hall
Buffalo, New York

In 1927 John Wade described his proposed design for the Buffalo City Hall as reflecting "the new spirit of originality in American architecture which is one of the outstanding features of this generation. The dependence on European tradition is rapidly waning in this country, where an entirely different set of circumstances must be faced. Utility, logic and harmony between the purposes for which a building is erected and the design of its structure are paramount." Fortunately, the building's originality was in no way suppressed for the sake of utility, logic or harmony. A half century after completion, Wade's building, with its zigzag ornamentation, stripped classicism, verticality and heroic murals, skylight and sculpture, is considered one of the best examples of Art Deco architecture in the United States. In retrospect, it is apparent that much of what Wade thought of as American originality was derived from Paris's 1925 Exposition Internationale des Arts Décoratifs et Industriels Modernes, for the building's chevron ornamentation and the polygonal shape of the dome recall the shapes popular at the Paris exposition. But the building's robustness and its siting at the most important of Buffalo's baroque intersections—Niagara Square, with its Carrère and Hastings monument (1907) to President William McKinley, assassinated in 1901 while attending Buffalo's Pan-American Exposition— give the structure a vitality and durability seldom achieved in 20th-century municipal architecture. Buffalo's city plan dates to Joseph Ellicott's layout of 1804. Approximately 100 years later, Daniel Burnham conceived the general concept for the development of Niagara Square. Dietel and Wade, a Buffalo architectural firm, was commissioned to design the city hall, with Wade the primary designer. Sullivan Jones, a New York City architect, was brought into the project at the insistence of the city council. Bryant Baker carved the statues of Presidents Fillmore and Cleveland, while Albert T. Stewart, Rene P. Chambellan and Graf and McIleen were responsible for the building's sculpture. The murals were painted by William de Leftwich Dodge and local craftsmen.

1929–31. Dietel and Wade; Sullivan W. Jones
65 Niagara Square (Erie County)
National Register of Historic Places

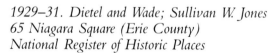

Schenectady City Hall
Schenectady, New York

Forty years after McKim, Mead and White initiated the Georgian Revival style of architecture and at least 10 years after any of the founders had been active practitioners, the firm designed this Georgian Revival building for Schenectady. Full of pleasing revival features—details such as the cupola, garlands and pilasters; the contrast of white stone and red brick; and handsomely decorated public spaces—the building's only unusual feature is the curved elevation. Costing more than a million dollars, the building has a lavishly decorated white marble main stair hall, council chamber and courtroom. The conservatism of the design reflects more than the tastes of the client and the firm, which won this commission in an invitational competition during the Depression, for other cities also erected architecturally safe, perhaps psychologically comforting Georgian Revival city halls, recalling the earlier days of the nation. The building was constructed on the site partly occupied by the much smaller 1880 city hall. Schenectady had simply outgrown its 19th-century city hall its population had increased from 12,000 people in the 1880s to 88,000 in 1920, many of whom worked for Schenectady's two booming companies—General Electric Company and American Locomotive. The current structure is unaltered and continues to serve as the city hall. In general style, the city hall echoes the adjacent 1912 post office, designed by James Knox Taylor. But the post office facade lacks the pleasing contrast of colors found in the city hall.

1930–31. McKim, Mead and White
100 Jay Street (Schenectady County)
National Register of Historic Places

Tacoma Municipal Administration Building

Tacoma, Washington

The skyscrapers of the 1930s, such as Tacoma's recently converted former Medical Arts Building, can be described by a number of stylistic terms including "stripped classicism," "Art Deco," "zigzag moderne" and "modernistic." The variety of classifications points out the lack of consensus among architectural historians as to whether they are talking about an architectural or decorative style. This building established that Art Deco is a decorative style applied to architecture, with an overwhelming emphasis on decoration. The concern with architecture, with working in all three dimensions, is limited in this structure to the setbacks and the deep, tall entrance. By contrast, the concern with decoration is expressed throughout the building in the wide variety of decorative shapes and colors. A variety of naturalistic Mayan and Aztec and geometric motifs relieves the otherwise unornamented exterior surfaces. Beginning with the rose tavernelle marble foyers with bronze grilles, the interior offers a plethora of luxuriant colors. The lobby, with its golden ceiling and bronze and glass light fixtures, leads to the three-story black granite staircase with bronze balustrades. The bronze elevator doors are framed by black granite surrounds. The wall and ceiling decorations in the public spaces juxtapose strong colors, strong shapes and exotic materials, creating a striking visual tapestry. The lead architect was John Graham of Seattle, who, as former chief architect for Ford Motor Company, had designed more than 30 plants. Heath, Gove and Bell was a nationally known firm, headquartered in Tacoma. In July 1977 the city of Tacoma purchased the building for use as a city hall. The architectural firm of Pearson and Richards has converted the building's auditorium into the city council chamber, opened up five floors to create office space, updated mechanical systems and replaced windows. Tacoma's previous city hall has been converted to shops.

1930–31. John Graham, Sr.; Heath, Gove and Bell
Medical Arts Building, Tacoma Rhodes Tower
740 St. Helen's Avenue (Pierce County)
National Register of Historic Places

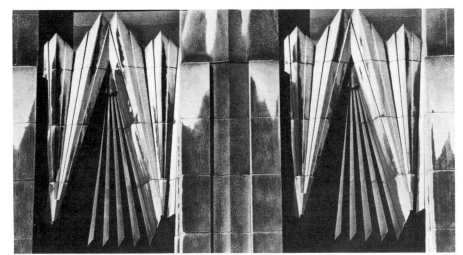

159

St. Paul City Hall and Ramsey County Courthouse
St. Paul, Minnesota

By the mid-1920s, St. Paul's city hall was too small to meet the needs of both city and county, so a new city hall was proposed. In 1927 a courthouse and city hall commission was established; it decided that the new building would be a collaboration between a St. Paul architect and an architect with a national practice. All St. Paul architects and several nonresident architects were invited to appear before the commission. The Chicago-based but national firm of Holabird and Root was awarded responsibility for the basic design, while Ellerbe and Company developed the design concept. An architect's rendering of St. Paul City Hall portrayed a stark, virtually windowless building with a strong verticality created by a series of low setbacks and continuous, dark vertical strips (actually windows). As constructed, the building looks less like a futuristic grain storage elevator than the rendering suggested. The building's monolithic exteriors are relieved by a few bas-reliefs by Lee Lawrie. Inside the Fourth Street entrance is Memorial Hall, a long, dark passage culminating in the three-story onyx sculpture *Indian God of Peace,* by Carl Milles. In contrast to the marble surfaces of Memorial Hall, the council chamber is paneled in English oak and California walnut and has four large murals by John Norton depicting St. Paul's history and its laborers. Similar themes are expressed in the elevator doors' bas-reliefs by E. R. Stewart. As in Tacoma's city hall, the Art Deco style is used here to create a powerful architectural image. The starkness of the exteriors contrasts with the interior spaces, which are luxuriously decorated with imported marbles and woods. Futuristic details include the revolving stand for Milles's sculpture and stylized fixtures and signage. Thirty-five percent of the building's space is used by the city and 65 percent by the county.

1930–31. Holabird and Root; Ellerbe and Company
15 West Kellogg Boulevard (Ramsey County)

Lynchburg City Hall
Lynchburg, Virginia

By the time this post office and courthouse was erected, the federal government seemed to have lost its ability to build inspired classical revival architecture, at least in Lynchburg. This lackluster edifice, with its flat facades and commonplace details, seems to mirror the state of the country during the Depression and of much Depression-era government architecture. It certainly does not reflect the ability of Stanhope Johnson, Lynchburg's accomplished revivalist architect. Johnson's design was modified slightly by James A. Wetmore, a lawyer who was supervising architect of the U.S. Treasury Department from 1915 to 1933. One of the two important public buildings constructed in Lynchburg during the 1930s, this structure appears unexciting partly because it is directly across the street from a more impressive building, a former city hall and post office designed by James Knox Taylor. Johnson's building, which was occupied by the federal government from 1933 to 1980, has been gutted and renovated by the architectural firm of Fauber Garbee for use as the city hall. It also houses a branch library and cable television studio.

1932–33. Stanhope Johnson; James A. Wetmore
U.S. Post Office and Court House
900 Church Street

Miami City Hall
Miami, Florida

Miami City Hall is a good example of adaptive use, a better example of 1930s architecture and perhaps the best extant example of an early air terminal. After being used as a terminal for 11 years, the Pan American Airways System Terminal Building at Dinner Key served as a marina office and restaurant for four years and as a city hall since 1954. The building was designed by Delano and Aldrich, an important early 20th-century architectural firm whose other commissions included the Post Office Department building in Washington, D.C., John D. Rockefeller estate at Pocantico Hills, N.Y., and Walters Art Gallery in Baltimore. The building is designed in the 1930s streamlined moderne architectural style, considered especially appropriate for air terminals and other structures relating to high-speed travel. The building also played an important role in the development of air travel. At the time of construction, the Pan American Airways terminal was the largest and most modern air terminal in the world. With its unprecedented ability to handle four seaplanes simultaneously, it was the nation's busiest commercial terminal, linking traffic between North and South America. It was also the model for terminals in San Francisco, New York and Rio de Janeiro. The structure is approached by a wide, landscaped boulevard; to the sides are hangars converted for use as an auditorium, convention hall and buildings for boat storage and repair. On the waterfront behind the terminal is a marina. Although the general configuration of the buildings has been retained and the original PanAm symbols remain, the building has undergone major alterations. In 1951 architect Robert Law Weed modified the windows, doors and canopy, as well as the interior. In 1953 architect M. M. Variloff replaced many of the original windows and doors and enclosed the two-story lobby to provide office space. Two small additions were erected in 1958. Also during the 1950s, the lobby murals were covered or painted over and the glass-block windows added.

1933–34. Delano and Aldrich
Pan American Airways System Terminal Building, Marina Building
3500 Pan American Drive (Dade County)

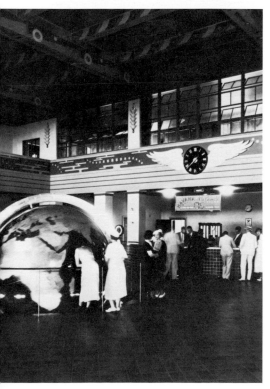

163

Kansas City City Hall

Kansas City, Missouri

This structure is the dominant building of a three-building complex, construction of which was approved by the people of Kansas City in 1931. The construction program, known as the Ten-Year Plan, symbolized stability, progress and faith in the future and helped counter the effects of the Depression. The building's architecture, although Beaux-Arts in plan and stripped classical in elevation, introduces Art Deco elements in its ornamentation. The stylized, naturalistic and mechanistic decorations typical of the 1930s are abundantly applied to the building's public spaces, such as the lobby and city council chamber. Exterior decoration is limited primarily to the six-story base, which features heroic figures at the cornice level. The metal spandrels and five-story, recessed entrance are ornamented with metal decorations. Each of the building's setbacks has bas-relief sculpture at its corners or cornice level. The architects designed the sculptures, which were executed by C. P. Jennewein, Ulric H. Ellerhusen and Walker Hancock. Directly south of the building is a stepped, formal plaza that separates the city hall from the Jackson County Courthouse, also designed by Wight and Wight, a Kansas City firm. This firm also designed the police headquarters, the third building in the 1931 construction program, which is east of the plaza.

1936–37. Wight and Wight
414 East 12th Street (Jackson County)

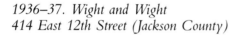

Davidson County Public Building and Court House
Nashville, Tennessee

On first observation, Nashville's city hall looks like a neoclassical municipal building built during the first two decades of the 20th century. Its major facade has a typical row of multistory columns on a high base, and the raised platform in front of the building has two fountains placed with Beaux-Arts symmetry. Closer inspection, however, reveals stylized Art Deco decoration in the spandrels and cornice; moreover, the entrances have the height, depth and heroic sculpture typical of the 1930s. And like other Art Deco municipal buildings, the highly decorated interior more than compensates for the relative austerity of the exterior. In fact, this building's exterior and interior ornamentation seems even more flamboyant and idiosyncratic than that of other contemporary public buildings. Frederic Hirons, of New York City, and Emmons Woolwine, of Nashville, had both been students at the Ecole des Beaux-Arts in Paris and collaborated to win the competition for this building, constructed as the Davidson County Court House. Undertaken with support from the Public Works Administration, the building was used for courts, with space rented to the city, since the local government had outgrown its existing facilities. In 1963 the city and county governments merged, forming the Metropolitan Government of Nashville and Davidson County. The building is the fourth courthouse built on Nashville's Public Square, which has been reserved since the 1780s for public buildings. The exterior sculpture above the doors, by an unknown artist, depicts Moses, Justinian, King John and blindfolded Justice. The figures flanking the doors represent Courage, Loyalty, Law, Justice, Security and Wisdom, as do the figures in the cornice. Faced in red-brown Tennessee marble with brass elevator doors and bronze stair rails, the entrance lobby has murals, by Dean Cornwall, of heroic figures representing Industry, Agriculture, Commerce and Statesmanship. The lobby's ceiling is a painted sunburst illuminated by a bronze-and-glass chandelier, each of whose panels is etched with a zodiac symbol. The exterior is unaltered except for the addition in 1981 of a ramp for the handicapped. In 1974 the council chamber suffered the loss of oak paneling, original pilasters and lighting fixtures, replaced with lowered ceilings, recessed lighting and smaller pilasters. The courtrooms have been altered at the discretion of the judges occupying them.

1936–37. Frederic C. Hirons; Emmons H. Woolwine
Public Square (Davidson County)

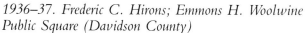

Houston City Hall

Houston, Texas

Houston's fourth city hall burned in 1904, yet it took 35 years for the city to build a fifth one. The Depression, as well as controversies concerning the site, architectural style and architect, interfered to delay the project. Not until 1913 did the city council agree that the proposed city hall would not be located on the site of its predecessors but opposite Hermann Square. From 1913 until the stock market crash of 1929, Hare and Hare, landscape architects and planners from Kansas City, prepared three plans for a city hall as the nucleus of a civic center. In the first plan, the buildings were neoclassical, with the city hall's design based on that of the U.S. Capitol. The second scheme showed the five buildings in a Spanish Renaissance Revival style and was accepted by the city planning commission in 1928. James Ruskin Baily, Alfred C. Finn and Hedrick and Gottlieb were commissioned to design the city hall. In 1929 they submitted their design, but the proposal, instead of being in the expected Spanish Renaissance Revival style, called for a 22-story skyscraper similiar to Los Angeles's city hall (1926–28) and the Nebraska State Capitol (1922–26, Bertram Goodhue). The Depression ended any hopes of financing the project, which remained dormant until 1937, when the Public Works Administration agreed to provide half the cost of the building. The city decided to proceed with the project, and a new architect, Joseph Finger, was retained. The mayor objected, on the grounds that the city had an obligation to retain the original architects and because he disliked Finger's contemporary design. Finger was an Austrian-born architect working in Houston who built a reputation for his streamlined, moderne buildings, such as Temple Beth Israel (1925) and TurnVerein Clubhouse (1929), both in Houston. The building's exterior ornamentation includes bas-relief sculpture near the top of setbacks and above the entrance, as well as decorated metal panels and grilles. The lobby has allegorical murals by Daniel MacMorris and streamlined modern metal and glass fixtures that are also found in the building's other public spaces. The major facade is on axis with a long reflecting pool in Hermann Square, all part of the civic center conceived by Hare and Hare. Directly behind the city hall is the 1968 annex. Alterations to the city hall itself have been limited to the mechanical systems. In 1982 the council chamber was renovated by Morris Aubry Architects, but the room's original appearance has been maintained.

1938–39. Joseph Finger
901 Bagby Street (Harrison County)

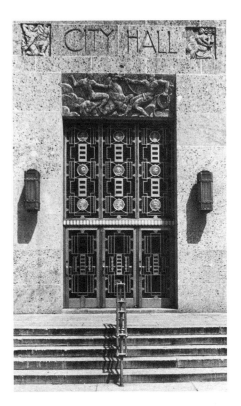

Oklahoma City Municipal Building
Oklahoma City, Oklahoma

Oklahoma City's municipal building blends Art Deco decorations with lingering neoclassicism. The main block has classical, fluted pilasters supporting an entablature, while the wings are decorated with Art Deco motifs. On the interior, similar ornamentation is used on capitals, grilles and lamps. Also characteristic of Art Deco city hall decoration is the use of several—in this case, seven—types of marble. The third-floor council chamber has 10-foot-high marble walls; above the marble is shell stone that extends to the ceiling. In contrast, the walls leading to the third-floor offices of the mayor and city manager are paneled with American black walnut. The municipal building is part of a four-building government complex that includes the county courthouse, municipal auditorium, city police headquarters and jail. The complex, partially funded by the Public Works Administration, Work Projects Administration and the Civil Works Administration, was built on the site of railroad tracks and a depot. The site had been purchased by the city from the Rock Island and Frisco railroads to relieve the traffic congestion caused by having a railroad depot and tracks in the heart of the city. Changes to the building have been limited to lowering ceilings for air-conditioning ducts, adding temporary walls and constructing a press box in the rear of the council chamber.

1936. Allied Architects
200 North Walker Street (Oklahoma County)

Lafayette City Hall

Lafayette, Louisiana

Built as the first Sears, Roebuck store in the area, this structure was enlarged in 1956 to two stories, linked by Lafayette's first escalator. The site originally was the plantation of one of Lafayette's earliest residents; later it was the location of a Carmelite monastery, which was supplanted by the Sears store. The Sears building was virtually a windowless, irregular box surrounded by vast parking lots—hardly an appropriate symbol for local government. Meleton-Patin-Guillory, the architectural firm responsible for the 1979–80 conversion for use as the city hall, sought to soften the building's stark facades. Energy conservation concerns and a limited budget, however, prevented the creation of windows. The architects were able to add a canopied entrance, skylighted central atrium and plantings to make the building more inviting to the public and a more appealing place in which to work. The work area's open space is divided by low partitions. This building is the second commercial structure Lafayette has successfully converted for use as a city hall.

1956–57. George L. Dahl and Associates
Sears, Roebuck Department Store
705 West University Avenue (Lafayette Parish)

Paducah City Hall

Paducah, Kentucky

When the Paducah-McCracken Development Council proposed a new city hall as part of a federally funded urban renewal project, it directed local architect Lee Potter Smith to suggest a prominent architect for its design. A week later Smith informed the council that Edward D. Stone was "eminently qualified" and that his design would be "contemporary and at the same time warm." Stone's proposal was not warm, but it was contemporary, being quite similar to his designs for many of his other clients. Paducah City Hall, the Kennedy Center (1971) and the U.S. Pavilion for the Brussels World's Fair (1958) are all based on his New Delhi Embassy (1954). Stone made his early reputation as an International Style architect through such commissions as the Museum of Modern Art (1936, with Philip Goodwin) and the Mandel House (1936), Mt. Kisco, N.Y. In his later works, he favored white buildings faced in marble, with wide overhangs supported by a colonnade (unless the building was a skyscraper) and with an interior courtyard. Paducah's city hall varies from the norm in two regards: Cost overruns necessitated the substitution of exposed aggregate panels for Italian travertine marble on the exterior, and Stone used an unusual pyramid skylight above the central atrium. This structure demonstrates Stone's ability to create a strong sense of verticality, through the use of continuous vertical window strips, in a low, horizontal building with an overhang. In 1970 a plaza and fountain proposed by Stone but designed by landscape architects Scruggs and Hammonds were built, linking the city hall, county courthouse and public library.

1963–65. Edward Durell Stone; Lee Potter Smith and Associates
South Fifth Street (McCracken County)

Boston City Hall
Boston, Massachusetts

Under a 1961 master plan by I. M. Pei and Partners, Boston's dilapidated Scollay Square was cleared, to be replaced with a federally funded urban renewal complex consisting of federal, state and local government buildings, as well as some private ones. The new city hall, with its dramatic inverted-pyramid shape and vast plaza, is the focus of this complex, which also includes the Government Service Center (1969, Paul Rudolph) and the John F. Kennedy Federal Building (1962, Architects Collaborative). The design, which was the winning entry in a national competition, has been praised by architectural critics for its boldness and exterior articulation of function. The offices where usual city hall business is conducted are located below ground; the plaza's brick paving is continued into the structure, up a raised plaza that is used for ceremonies. Several feet above the plaza are suspended concrete bays housing the mayor's office, council chamber and offices for council members. Above these bays are the floors occupied by the city government employees. Considered the symbol of Boston's renewal, this structure and its plaza are also intimately linked to Boston's past. Directly east is the 18th-century Faneuil Hall and 19th-century Quincy Market. The restored 19th-century Sears Crescent buildings define, in part, the southern edge of the city hall plaza. When Kallmann, McKinnell and Knowles won the city hall competition they were unknown architects, teaching at Columbia University. Kallman and McKinnell subsequently moved to Boston, forming with Henry Wood a national architectural practice. The Boston City Hall competition demonstrates the usefulness of competitions in generating unusual designs and in launching careers for previously unknown architects.

1963–69. Kallmann, McKinnell and Knowles; Campbell, Aldrich and Nulty
1 City Hall Square (Suffolk County)

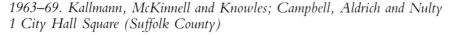

Scottsdale City Hall

Scottsdale, Arizona

Built in a declining downtown section, this city hall is part of the Scottsdale civic center, which also includes the courts, public safety buildings, library and the Scottsdale Center for the Arts. The civic center was an urban renewal project instigated by a citizens group, the Scottsdale Town Enrichment Program (STEP), that wanted to counter the deterioration of the downtown. These buildings are set in a plaza with sculpture, lush vegetation, fountains and manicured lawns bordered by pedestrian paths. The city hall, designed by Bennie M. Gonzales Associates, a Scottsdale architectural firm, is a masonry and concrete evocation of the native American architectural traditions of the Southwest. The entrance and lobby open directly into the sunken council chamber. On the mezzanine around the chamber are the administrative offices and balconies for overflow crowds to observe council proceedings. Stained-glass skylights by Glidden Parker, a Scottsdale artist, light the council chamber, which is the building's focus. To emphasize the chamber's importance and the Indian heritage, the space has been designated the Kiva, the Hopi term for a partially submerged ceremonial structure. The Scottsdale Civic Center has received national attention as a sensitive blending of the community's history, civic needs and contemporary architecture.

1968. Bennie M. Gonzales Associates
Civic Center Plaza (Maricopa County)

Kettering Government Center
Kettering, Ohio

Incorporated in 1955 and named in honor of automative pioneer and philanthropist Charles F. Kettering, Kettering was a rapidly growing city in search of an identity when it undertook the building of a government center in the 1960s. The pyramid-shaped city hall was intended to be a symbol of the municipality and of the council form of government. As one city councilman noted, the Kettering government "wanted a symbol of its progressive spirit as well as a community focal point. . . . The two-story space in the center of the pyramid accommodates a spacious, open council chamber. The roof lines translate the chamber's signficance to the exterior, and a large opening through the roof structure announces the chamber's presence to any person approaching the building." Kettering's city hall shares its heavily wooded 8-acre site with the complementary and intentionally less dramatic justice building, designed by Lorenz-Williams-Williams-Lively and Likens and built in 1973. Eugene W. Betz Architects, whose office is in Kettering, was picked from 32 architects who had expressed an interest in designing the new municipal building.

1968–69. Eugene W. Betz Architects
3600 Shroyer Road (Montgomery County)

Tempe Municipal Building
Tempe, Arizona

The city of Tempe and the architects commissioned to design the new city hall give compelling reasons for the choice of location and the building's shape. The city council chose the site, near Tempe's central business district, to express confidence in the downtown area. The inverted-pyramid shape is, according to the architects, based on the client's needs and the constraints of Arizona's climate. The architects, a Tempe firm, wrote that "the program for administrative offices determined an increased area at each successively higher level. The resulting space volume, rotated 45 degrees, provided maximum sunlight in the garden and maximum summer shade upon the sloping glass walls of the building, significantly reducing air conditioning load. An ageless quality was sought in the pure geometry of the building." The architects' explanation makes the building's design seem solely practical, but it seems hardly coincidental that Tempe, along with Kettering, Boston and Dallas, would need pyramid-derived designs for their city halls to satisfy their programmatic needs. That so many major city hall commissions of the 1960s and 1970s were unusual, dramatically shaped buildings suggests that the value of the building as a symbol of the city was given prominence over more mundane design issues.

1969–71. Michael and Kemper Goodwin
31 East Fifth Street (Maricopa County)

Fairfield City Hall

Fairfield, California

Neither this building nor the other structures in Fairfield's 33-acre civic center is a landmark building. But as an ensemble, the buildings create a harmonious and inviting complex, organized around a 3-acre artifical lake. Besides the usual administrative buildings, the civic center has a 750-seat assembly hall and a community center, a multiuse facility for recreational and cultural activities. The city leaders desired and achieved in the civic center a complex for the public enjoyment, not simply an undistinguished office building that happens to be city hall. In the spirit of democratic, open government, the architect for the civic center project was selected by means of a competition open to all registered architects in northern and central California. In addition, the city council meets in a separate, one-story, sloped-roof building with a largely glass facade; thus, the public can easily observe city council proceedings. Fairfield's acquisition of public art for the various buildings reiterates the concept that public buildings are for the public's use and enjoyment.

1969–71. Robert W. Hawley, AIA
1000 Webster Street (Solano County)

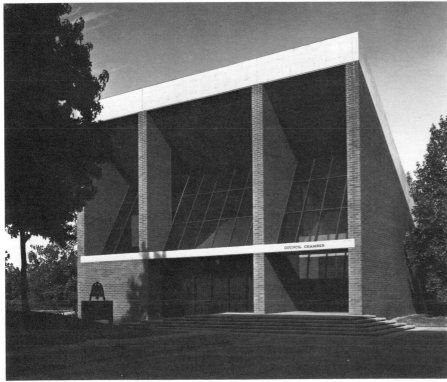

181

San Bernardino City Hall
San Bernardino, California

This structure is the focus of the 11-acre San Bernardino Civic Cultural Center, which, in turn, is part of a 93-acre downtown urban renewal project carried out in the mid-1970s. Bounded by the cultural center's parking garage, a theater and commercial buildings, the city hall has bronze-tinted glass panels with dark bronze spandrels; even the columns have bronzed aluminum covers. Despite the building's uniform, gridlike appearance, substantial accommodations have been made for the sun's effect and movement. The majority of offices are on the building's north side, which has transparent glass panels. The east and west sides have few offices and small windows made of opaque panels. The south side has opaque glass–faced panels and houses service spaces. This building reflects the experimentation with proportion, color and shape that is typical of the work of Cesar Pelli, who was Gruen Associates' principal designer and is now dean of the Yale University School of Architecture. The Argentina-born architect has emerged as one of the most important architects of the late 1970s and the 1980s; he has designed the Pacific Design Center, Los Angeles, the renovation and tower of the Museum of Modern Art and Battery City Park, New York City, all currently under construction.

1972. Cesar Pelli, Gruen Associates
300 North D Street (San Bernardino County)

Dallas City Hall
Dallas, Texas

"Dallas City Hall had to be more than just an office building," concluded architect I. M. Pei about this 560-foot-long and 122-foot-high concrete trapezoidal building. "We had to be concerned about people's perception of what the building should be. We chose to make it long and low because we felt it should contrast with private institutional buildings. There was another reason for making it low. A public building has to have a public space, just as in front of a cathedral there's always a square. If you put a tower in front of a plaza, the plaza leaks everywhere, and you end up with no enclosures. A low building embraces the plaza and makes it its own. So the search for the symbolic is very important in this context." The cantilevered facade of the city hall, sited on a 4-acre plaza, faces north. The sculpture in front of the building, by Henry Moore, was created for this space. The building's most interesting interior feature is the great court, which extends the length of the building at the third level and is lighted by three skylights approximately 100 feet above. Ada Louise Huxtable, former architecture critic of the *New York Times*, praised the building as bold and monumental. She also noted that only Boston's government center, designed also by Pei, with its handsome, bold city hall, could compare to Dallas's Municipal Administration Center as an urban grouping. Pei, recipient of the AIA Gold Medal and the Pritzker Architectural Prize, also designed the John Hancock Tower (1973), Boston, the National Gallery of Art East Building (1979), Washington, D.C., and the John Fitzgerald Kennedy Library (1979), Boston.

1972–77. I.M. Pei and Partners; Harper and Kemp
Municipal Administration Center (Dallas County)

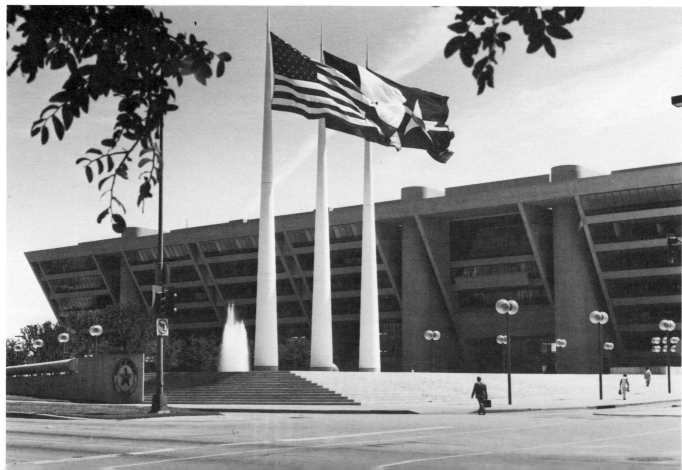

Wilmington City-County Building
Wilmington, Delaware

Wilmington's new city-county building is an integral part of a civic complex comprising federal, state and local government offices and privately owned buildings. The complex was envisioned as a major element in Wilmington's long-term urban renewal plans to counter downtown deterioration. Because both the city and county governments had outgrown their joint 1914–17 facility and offices had been dispersed throughout the city, a new city-county building was approved. Wilmington's new city-county building, a starkly modern structure, is consistent with the architectural trend of viewing public buildings as primarily administrative spaces. According to this view, the most efficient design is a nondescript highrise office building that could just as easily house lawyers and accountants as city employees. The design of Wilmington's city-county building makes two major concessions to the fact that a city office building is a public building: First, much effort has been put into the public spaces such as the council chamber and the two-story lobby, which displays art and sculpture exhibits and two permanent works of art, one a WPA mural. Second, the council chamber is housed in a masonry-and-glass annex separate from the other offices, thus indicating the symbolic nature of the council's function. It appears that only a few cities—Boston, Dallas, Kettering and Tempe—are willing to build more dramatically shaped city halls that display art and sculpture exhibits.

1975–77. Vincent G. Kling and Partners; Whiteside, Moeckel and Carbonell
800 French Street (New Castle County)

Springfield City Hall
Springfield, Ohio

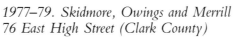

This city hall was conceived by a citizens task force as a vehicle for invigorating a blighted downtown. The expectation that a new government building would encourage the rehabilitation of existing structures and businesses and attract new ones to the area has been fulfilled. With its setbacks, placement on the diagonal and open central bays on the first floor, the building appears to be an extension of its plaza. The result is that the plaza seems larger and the building more inviting to the public. At the central bays are two entrances, one to the council chamber, the other to the city offices. Skidmore, Owings and Merrill, the world's largest architectural firm, is most often associated with large-scale, multimillion dollar projects such as the Sears Tower (1974), Chicago, U.S. Air Force Academy (1963), Colorado Springs, and Haj Terminal (1982), Jeddah, Saudi Arabia. This city hall is an example of the firm's ability to design more modest structures that have a human scale, relate well to the surrounding public spaces and create an appropriate symbol of local government. The modern movement in architecture, of which Skidmore, Owings and Merrill has been a major proponent, has been faulted for designing buildings that are insensitive to users and surroundings and that exacerbate rather than reduce society's problems. Springfield's city hall demonstrates some of the positive qualities of modern architecture.

1977–79. Skidmore, Owings and Merrill
76 East High Street (Clark County)

CITY HALL FEATURES

CITY HALL

Domes and Rotundas

The dome is one of the most sophisticated and powerful images in architecture. City hall architects have used domes to connote the institutional nature of the building and to call attention to the structure. The rotunda beneath the dome is the hub of the building, organizing circulation horizontally and, often, vertically.

above
Savannah City Hall (1904–05, Hyman W. Witcover) has a complex dome consisting of railings, lantern and pediments facing north, south, east and west, thereby continuing the vertical emphasis of the main mass of the building.

left
Pasadena City Hall (1926–27, John Bakewell, Jr., and Arthur Brown, Jr.) has a massive dome, covered with red fish-scale tiles, that was intended to dominate the city's skyline.

above
San Francisco City Hall (1913–15, John Bakewell, Jr., and Arthur Brown, Jr.) has a dome whose scale and intricacy of detailing compete with those of the U.S. Capitol and St. Peter's Cathedral in Rome.

right, top and bottom
Baltimore City Hall (1867–75, George A. Frederick) exhibits relatively little detailing in its dome, yet it makes a strong visual statement conveying a sense of movement evident throughout the rotunda.

Towers

Towers were built on city halls ostensibly to display bells or clocks, but such public-service functions only hint at the most obvious of their purposes. Towers of city halls and churches rose above the 19th-century cityscape, calling attention to the building. Corner towers on city halls anchored intersections, giving the city hall a dominance over other buildings facing the intersection. With the elimination of towers in post–Richardsonian architecture, city hall architects lost one of the most effective means of drawing attention to the building and conveying its importance to the community.

opposite, left
New York City Hall (1803–11, John McComb, Jr., and Joseph Francois Mangin) culminates in a finely detailed Federal-style tower with coupled corner columns and urns. The tower is topped with a high cupola with a sculpture of Justice.

opposite, top
Chicopee City Hall (1871, Charles Edward Parker) counters the normal expectation that a tower narrows at its top. Instead, this tower spreads out and then in, finally terminating in a bird weathervane.

opposite, middle
Springfield City Hall, Mass. (1909–13, F. Livingston Pell and Harvey Wiley Corbett), has a bell tower whose design evokes the spirit and form of early European city hall towers.

opposite, bottom
Lancaster Municipal Building (1891–92, James H. Windrim) might have been built in the Southwest, for its tower suggests the baroque architecture of the colonies settled by the Spanish, rather than the simple medieval architecture of the colonies settled by the British.

above and right
Philadelphia City Hall (1871–1901, John McArthur, Jr., and Thomas U. Walter) builds to a dramatic summit with a tower topped by a sculpture by Alexander Milne Calder of William Penn, stretching his hand out over the city he founded.

Skylights

Skylights are almost as integral to city halls as stained-glass windows are to churches. In many 19th- and early 20th-century city halls, a skylight illuminated the major interior space while exaggerating its height. Through the use of stained glass, the skylights added additional color to the rooms and focused visitors' attention. Some recent city halls continue the use of skylights, but they tend to be simpler and more abstract than earlier designs.

opposite
Yonkers City Hall (1907–10, H. Lansing Quick) has so much surface decoration that in rooms such as the council chamber it would be disjointed and confusing except that the skylight serves as the focus of the ornamentation and helps unify it.

above
Buffalo City Hall (1929–31, Dietel and Wade; Sullivan W. Jones), with its exquisitely detailed and colored ornamentation, such as the skylight in the city council chamber, conveys the richness and imagination that made Art Deco such an exciting architectural style in the 1930s.

right
Cleveland City Hall (1912–14, J. Milton Dyer) has a Great Hall crowned by a skylight; the walls are made of Bottincini marble from Italy.

left
North Little Rock City Hall (1914, John L. Howard) suggests the Art Nouveau delicacy of a Tiffany lamp or stained glass in the finely detailed, subtly colored stained-glass skylight.

left
Richmond Old City Hall (1886–94, Elijah E. Myers) has two large skylights, each consisting of several panes of glass. These not only light the large courtyards but also provide an upward focus for the interiors.

above
Scottsdale City Hall (1968, Bernie M. Gonzales Associates) suggests the Native American heritage in its design, primarily of the council chamber; the abstract, nonsymbolic skylights serve as a contrast.

right, above
Providence City Hall (1874–78, Samuel J. F. Thayer) has a skylight that is completely lacking in ornamentation, but its shape and length provide dramatic interest.

right
Little Rock City Hall (1907–08, Charles L. Thompson) has a baroque quality, for the visitor has a sense of moving upward until reaching the atrium, where the skylight draws the attention even further up.

Stairs and Atriums

City halls are striking for their strongly contrasting exterior and interior treatments. While the exteriors are often composed of massive, powerful masonry, indicating solidity and immensity, the interiors, often with smooth, polished surfaces, suggest movement and depth. The ornamentation, finish and proportions of the atrium stairway have changed many times since the 18th century, but this feature has remained the focus of the city hall and a means of avoiding static interiors.

above, top
The Cabildo (1795–99, Gilberto Guillemard) lacks the refined dignity of other city halls' stairs, but it has instead a solid, functional feel.

above, bottom
New York City Hall (1803–11, John Mc-Comb, Jr., and Joseph Francois Mangin) reflects the delicate, refined taste of the period as seen in the stairs' strong sense of movement.

left
Minneapolis City Hall and Courthouse (1889–1905, Long and Kees) has a hard, clean quality to its interior; the surfaces of its large, tall atrium and stairs are polished to a hard smoothness.

above and right
Richmond Old City Hall (1886–94,
Elijah E. Myers) is an elaborate, powerful evocation of the Gothic; the upward
lift of the pointed arches is strongly reinforced by the steep, wide stairs.

above
Lowell City Hall (1890–93, Merrill and Cutler) creates a tension in its interior between the tensile, tactile quality of its metal stair balustrades and the substantial, compressed quality of the stone columns supporting the stairs.

left
St. Louis City Hall (1890–1904, George Richard Mann; Harvey Ellis; Albert B. Groves) set the standard for atriums and stairs with its forceful demonstration that a large atrium can retain a human scale and yet be a powerful space.

above and right, top
Providence City Hall (1874–78, Samuel J. F. Thayer) achieves a rare balance between the nearly overwhelming sweep of its stairs and the tranquillity of its stair landings.

opposite, above
Bay City City Hall (1894–97, Pratt and Koeppe) has soaring staircases whose entire surfaces are embellished, a feature possible only in the post–Civil War period because of the introduction of precast metal.

right
Boston City Hall (1963–69, Kallmann, McKinnell and Knowles; Campbell, Aldrich and Nulty) creates visual interest in its interior, not through the use of detailing or expensive materials but by means of a stair and atrium that sweep the visitor up into the heart of the building.

201

Council Chambers

For most of the 19th century, city governments were controlled by city councils, which conducted their public business in chambers that, in size and decoration, reflected the council's power. These chambers were often large, multistory rooms in which the public was relegated to balconies or a separate, railed-off section. With the emergence of a strong mayoral form of government in the late 19th century and the commission and manager forms in the 20th century, council chambers have become less ornate, theoretically more democratic.

left
Cleveland City Hall (1912–14, J. Milton Dyer) has a council chamber rivaling those of the 19th century in terms of its sheer size, height and elaborate detailing.

opposite, top
Los Angeles City Hall (1926–28, John C. Austin, Albert C. Martin and John Parkinson) suggests in its design that by the time this city hall was built, power had shifted from the council to mayor. The council chamber lacks the height and grandeur of 19th-century council chambers.

opposite, middle
Kansas City City Hall (1936–37, Wight and Wight) has one of the most impressive council chambers of all 20th century city halls. The chamber artfully combines grandeur of height with strikingly intricate details.

opposite, bottom
Baltimore City Hall (1867–75, George A. Frederick) has a council chamber that displays the mid- to late 19th-century taste for heavy ornamentation such as that used in the door and window hoods.

right, top
Charleston City Hall (1800–01, attributed to Gabriel Manigault) conveys, in the small balcony area for public observation of council deliberations, the reality that when this building was constructed, government was by the elite and not the business of all the people.

right, bottom
Philadelphia City Hall (1871–1901, John McArthur, Jr., and Thomas U. Walter) has an exuberant exterior and some interior spaces, but the council chamber has a more restrained, dignified quality.

opposite
St. Louis City Hall (1890–1904, George Richard Mann; Harvey Ellis; Albert B. Groves) has an ornate but surprisingly intimate council chamber.

above
Lowell City Hall (1890–93, Merrill and Cutler) expresses in its council chamber the Richardsonian Romanesque style's appreciation of heavily paneled rich, dark woods.

right, top
Albany City Hall (1881–83, Henry Hobson Richardson) underwent substantial interior remodeling in 1919 by Ogden and Gander; thus, the council chamber, with its coffered ceiling and hanging lamps, reflects early 20th-century tastes rather than Richardson's design.

right, bottom
Rochester City Hall (1884–91, Harvey Ellis or Mifflin E. Bell) was not built as a city hall, so the council meets in what was once a suitably impressive, heavily paneled courtroom.

Murals

The use of murals to add color and fill wall space in city halls first became popular in the mid- to late 19th century. Murals reached their peak in the 1930s when they were often the major decoration; often they were larger-than-life depictions of early settlers and history. Later murals have been less realistic in style, dealing with less serious themes.

left, top
Lynchburg Old City Hall (1909–12, James Knox Taylor) is distinguished on the interior by a 1934 painting by Scaisbrooke L. Abbot, commissioned by the WPA. The mural, showing an oxcart transporting tobacco to market, depicts Lynchburg's early history as a tobacco town.

left, bottom
Trenton Municipal Building (1908–10, Spencer Roberts) has the distinction of having two murals by the important Ashcan School artist Everett Shinn, painted in 1911, which are different from the council chamber's original decorations but look appropriate in the room.

above, opposite and right
Davidson County Public Building and Court House, Nashville (1936–37, Frederic C. Hirons; Emmons H. Woolwine), is decorated with Art Deco–style murals—these by Dean Cornwall—intended to depict not only the economic basis of Tennessee but also its political and agrarian history.

right
Bay City City Hall (1894–97, Pratt and Koeppe) has a rather fanciful mural, created by Monika Chmielewska in 1980, in its council chamber, in marked contrast to the serious art usually seen in government buildings.

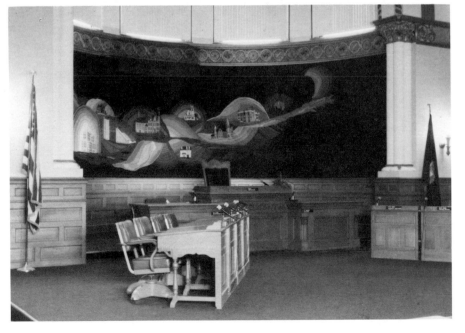

Sculpture

Sculpture in a city hall serves as a reminder that the building is a symbol of the community, its government and its history—all of which are often depicted in the sculpture. Sculpture by internationally prominent artists has given scale, detail and symbolism to city halls, from Carl Milles's sculpture *Indian God of Peace,* the focus of St. Paul City Hall's Memorial Hall, to Henry Moore's sculpture reposing in front of the Dallas City Hall to Alexander Calder's figures enlivening the face of Philadelphia City Hall.

208

opposite, top
Oakland City Hall (1911–14, Palmer and Hornbostel) was built for what was originally a farming community, and the grape sculpture recalls this history.

opposite, middle
Buffalo City Hall (1929–31, Dietel and Wade; Sullivan W. Jones) has on its lower stories sculpture by Albert T. Stewart depicting the industries of Buffalo. The emphasis is on manual labor, as was typical of WPA-era sculpture and contemporary sculpture in other countries.

opposite, bottom, left
University City City Hall (1903–04, Herbert C. Chivers) makes extensive use of sculpture, such as the goddesses flanking the impressive cantilevered stairs.

opposite, bottom, middle
Charleston City Hall (1800–01, attributed to Gabriel Manigault) was built as the U.S. Bank Branch with an eagle, the symbol of the federal government, in the pediment. When the building became the city hall, the eagle was replaced with the city seal.

above
Dallas City Hall (1972–77, I. M. Pei and Partners; Harper and Kemp), with its deeply cantilevered facade, creates a void in front of the building that is artfully filled by a Henry Moore sculpture.

opposite, bottom, right
Albany City Hall (1881–83, Henry Hobson Richardson) has, as part of the stringcourse, sculptures of gargoyles in dark stone; these provide contrast with the lighter colored walls and also break up the flat plane of the wall.

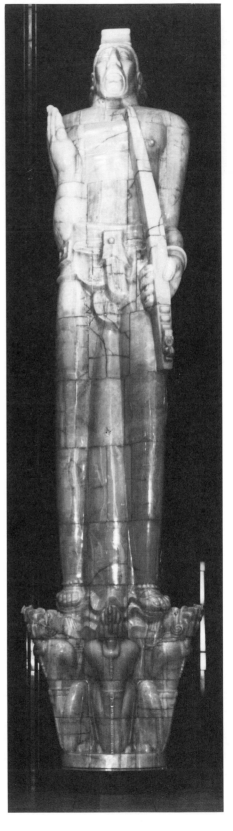

above and right
St. Paul City Hall and Ramsey County Courthouse (1930–31, Holabird and Root; Ellerbe and Company), like other city halls of the 1930s, used sculpture such as Lee Lawrie's relief to convey the activities considered important to the well-being of the community. Carl Milles's *Indian God of Peace* is used not only for ornamentation but as an essential design element.

left and above
Philadelphia City Hall (1871–1901, John McArthur, Jr., and Thomas U. Walter) was the world's tallest masonry-bearing structure when it was built, yet the sculpture at the roof level and even the William Penn sculpture topping the building, both by Alexander Milne Calder, are carefully detailed, although few would ever be close enough to appreciate the detailing.

Acknowledgments

America's City Halls would not have been possible without the aid of the staffs of the Historic American Buildings Survey and Historic American Engineering Record and the American Institute of Architects. Robert J. Kapsch, Chief of HABS/HAER, and S. Allen Chambers, Jr., architectural historian, provided invaluable criticisms of the manuscript. Alison K. Hoagland, Jet Lowe, Jack E. Boucher, Consuella Booth, Myra Jackson, Marlene Bergstrom, Jean Yearby and Paul Dolinsky also assisted in preparation of the manuscript. The American Institute of Architects has given generously of its time and money. A special debt is owed Maurice Payne, AIA, who has been involved in all aspects of this project. His colleagues in the AIA design program, along with Joy Brandon, Karen Vogel and Jim Ellison, AIA, provided valuable support. This manuscript was written in the AIA library, and I gratefully thank Stephanie Byrnes and her staff for their assistance. James Gasser helped conceive this project and made the initial contacts in carrying out this effort. I owe Karen Lebovich an immeasurable debt.

Many points made in the introduction were discussed with scholars, and I am indebted to Howard Gillette, Richard Bushman, William Wilson, Greer Hardwicke, Charles Goodsell, William Stull, Charles Glaab, Neil Harris and Mark Gelfand for their insight and advice. An additional acknowledgment is due Glaab, as many of the ideas in the introduction are from his and A. Theodore Brown's *A History of Urban America*.

I also wish to thank the Preservation Press, National Trust for Historic Preservation, for its assistance in working with HABS to develop and publish this book. *America's City Halls* was published under the direction of Diane Maddex, editor, Preservation Press books, and edited by Gretchen Smith, associate editor, with the assistance of Helen Cook and Christine Hosseinmardi, administrative assistants.

The historians who prepared the documentation on the individual city halls are listed here with the cities for which they provided information: *Annapolis, Md.*, Russell Wright, AIA; *Lancaster, Pa.* (Old City Hall), John J. Snyder, Jr.; *New Orleans, La.* (The Cabildo), Bayard T. Whitmore; *Wilmington, Del.* (Old Town Hall), Patricia D. Wilson, Patricia A. Maley, William E. Pelham, AIA, and John F. Haupt III, AIA; *Charleston, S.C.*, Margaretta P. Childs, Charles Bayless, AIA, and William D. Evans, AIA; *New York, N.Y.*, Marjorie Pearson; *Washington, D.C.* (Old City Hall), Nancy Schwartz, Diane Maddex and W. Brown Morton; *Salem, Mass.*, Allison Crump; *Brooklyn, N.Y.* (City Hall), Marjorie Pearson; *New Orleans, La.* (Gallier Hall), Bayard Whitmore; *Knoxville, Tenn.*, Gary Farlow, Ross Janney, Hester Fowler, Building Conservation Technology and Anderson Notter Finegold; *Norfolk, Va.* (Old City Hall and Courthouse), Virginia Historic Landmarks Commission, James Gehman, AIA, Lynda Stanley and Ralph Miner, Jr.; *Mobile, Ala.*, Elizabeth Gould, Roy Tallon and Nicholas Holmes, Jr., FAIA; *Wilmington, N.C.*, Joan Geiszler; *Petersburg, Va.*, Barbara Moore, Virginia Historic Landmarks Commission, John McRae and Randall Biallas; *Boston, Mass.* (Old City Hall), George Wrenn, Marcia Myers, Judy McDonough, Judy

Glasser and Ralph Memolo; *Salt Lake City, Utah* (City Hall), Linda Edeiken, AICP, Melvin Smith, George Adams and Paul Goeldner; *Baltimore, Md.*, Margaret Daiss, Nancy Miller and Arthur Townsend; *Norwich, Conn.*, Kate Ohno and Dale Plummer; *Chicopee, Mass.*, Alison Page; *Louisville, Ky.*, Susan McGowan and David Arbogast; *Alexandria, Va.*, Penny Morrill, Kim Heartwell, Gale Thompson and Suzanne Schell; *Philadelphia, Pa.*, Richard Tyler, John Maass, Carolyn Pitts and Patricia Siemiontkowski; *Providence, R.I.*, Joseph Chrostowski, Osmund Overby, Alice Hauk and Richard Harrington; *Lincoln, Neb.*, Daniel Kidd; *Brooklyn, N.Y.* (Flatbush Town Hall), Marjorie Pearson; *Albany, N.Y.*, Norman Rice, Chester Liebs and Cornelia Brooks; *Hoboken, N.J.*, Patricia Florio; *New Britain, Conn.*, Leland Roth, David Ransom, Anthony Aloisio and Sebastian Papa; *Lawrence, Kans.*, Robert Kosack, Tim Brown, Kirk McClure and Karen Goodell; *Rochester, N.Y.*, Kathryn Sette; *Richmond, Va.* (Old City Hall), John Albers, Virginia Historic Landmarks Commission; *Springfield, Ohio* (Old City Hall), Ann Armstrong and George Berkhofer; *San Antonio, Tex.*, Patricia Osborne; *Cincinnati, Ohio*, JoAnn Kurlemann and John Garner; *Cambridge, Mass.*, Daniel Reiff and Susan Maycock; *Syracuse, N.Y.*, Office of Federal and State Aid Coordination; *Lewiston, Maine*, Geneva Kirk and Gridley Barrows, AIA; *Minneapolis, Minn.*, Nancy Stanek, Steve Ristuben and William Scott; *Lowell, Mass.*, Robert Weible; *St. Louis, Mo.*, Division of Heritage and Urban Design, Department of Public Safety, City of St. Louis; *Lancaster, Pa.* (Municipal Building), John Snyder, Jr.; *Bellingham, Wash.* (New Whatcom City Hall), Richard Vanderway; *Salt Lake City, Utah* (City and County Building), Linda Edeiken; *Portland, Ore.*, Alfred Staehli, AIA, Wini Powers, Paul Hartwig and D. W. Powers III; *Brockton, Mass.*, Marian Hershenson, Christine Boulding and Robert Kane; *Las Vegas, N.M.*, Kathleen Brooker; *Milwaukee, Wis.*, Robin Wenger, John DeHaas, Jr., Mary Ellen Young and Richard Perrin; *Bay City, Mich.*, E. W. Kivisto; *Alameda, Calif.*, Gary Knecht and Sally Woodbridge; *Peoria, Ill.*, Les Kenyon, AIA, and Terry Kohlbuss; *Binghamton, N.Y.*, Clement Bowers, Eugene Montillon, Binghamton Commission on Architecture and Urban Design; *Lafayette, La.* (Old City Hall), Taylor Rock, Mario Mamalakis and M. L. Boulet; *Creston, Iowa*, Dennis Howard and Lawrence Ericsson, AIA; *Norfolk, Va.* (Old City Hall), James Gehman, AIA, Ralph Miner, Jr., Lynda Stanley and Virginia Historic Landmarks Commission; *Newark, N.J.*, Joseph Manning III; *University City, Mo.*, David Olson; *Savannah, Ga.*, Michael Vaquer, Jr., and Walton Bazemore, AIA; *Washington, D.C.* (The District Building), Ann Simpson-Mason; *Dayton, Ohio*, Teresa Prosser, Judy McCune and Fred Bartenstein; *Little Rock, Ark.*, Jacalyn Carfagno; *Yonkers, N.Y.*, Grinton Will, Jeanne Mikelson, Diana Koster and Kaeyer, Parker and Garment; *Berkeley, Calif.* (Old City Hall), Trish Hawthorne; *Trenton, N.J.*, Eric Drake, Daniel Vieyra and Rebecca Mitchell; *Indianapolis, Ind.*, Mary Ellen Gadski and James Glass; *Sacramento, Calif.*, Richard Hastings, Cynthia St. Louis, Art Gammel, AIA, and John Stafford, AIA; *Chicago, Ill.*, Ivar Viehe-Naess, Jr.; *Lynchburg, Va.* (Old City Hall), Liz Browning and S. Allen Chambers, Jr.; *Springfield, Mass.*, Margaret Lynch; *Pittsfield, Mass.*, Tony King; *Des Moines, Iowa*, Virgil Stanford, Jr., and Jack Porter; *Oakland, Calif.*, Kenneth Cardwell, FAIA; *Grand*

Forks, N.D., Norene Robert; *Cleveland, Ohio,* Thomas Ovington, AIA, Robert Gaede, AIA, Claire Rosacco, Edward Reich, Sue Kelly, John Cimperman and Robert Becker; *North Little Rock, Ark.,* Jacalyn Carfagno; *San Francisco, Calif.,* Joseph Baird, Henry Hope Reed and John and Sally Woodbridge; *Wilmington, Del.* (Public Building), Patricia Wilson, Patricia Maley, William Pelham, AIA, and John Haupt III, AIA; *Tampa, Fla.,* S. Keith Bailey, AIA; *Roanoke, Va.,* J. Oliver Stein; *Cheyenne, Wyo.,* Gerald Iverson; *Pittsburgh, Pa.,* Alan Tisdale, R.A.; *Littleton, Colo.,* Robert McQuarie and Veronica Ehlers; *Texarkana, Tex.,* Candy Stevens; *St. Joseph, Mo.,* Patricia Lawson; *Pasadena, Calif.,* Ann Scheid; *Los Angeles, Calif.,* Forrest Scott, AIA, Fred Croton, Richard Wurman, George Hales, David Gebhard and Robert Winter; *Gary, Ind.,* Gail Pugh and Carol-Ann Seaton; *Coral Gables, Fla.,* Carol Alper; *Duluth, Minn.,* Gene Gruba and Gerry Johnson; *Lexington, Mass.,* David Ostrow; *Phoenix, Ariz.,* Carl Craig; *Atlanta, Ga.,* Susan Gwinner; *Denver, Colo.,* Kenneth Fuller, AIA, and David Ballast; *Buffalo, N.Y.,* John Randall; *Schenectady, N.Y.,* Andrea Pollock and Doris Manley; *Tacoma, Wash.,* Karie Hayashi; *St. Paul, Minn.,* Seth Levin, Susan Ebner and Terry Pfoutz; *Lynchburg, Va.* (City Hall), Liz Browning and S. Allen Chambers, Jr.; *Miami, Fla.,* Sarah Eaton; *Kansas City, Mo.,* Thomas Bean; *Oklahoma City, Okla.,* Oklahoma Community Development Department and Bill Peavler, AIA; *Nashville, Tenn.,* Ann Reynolds; *Houston, Tex.,* Barrie Scardino; *Lafayette, La.* (City Hall), Taylor Rock, Mario Mamalakis and Pierce Meleton; *Paducah, Ky.,* J. Patrick Kerr, AIA; *Boston, Mass.* (City Hall), Marcia Myers, Judy McDonough, Judy Glasser and Ralph Memolo; *Scottsdale, Ariz.,* Janet Simmelink; *Kettering, Ohio,* Robert Makarius, Jr., AIA; *Tempe, Ariz.,* Maryanne Corder; *Fairfield, Calif.,* Jay Bodutch; *San Bernardino, Calif.,* Thelma Press, Vincent Bautista, Esther McCoy and Urban Land Institute; *Dallas, Tex.,* David Grubb and Peter Papademetriou; *Wilmington, Del.* (City-County Building), Patricia Wilson, Patricia Maley, William Pelham, AIA, and John Haupt III, AIA; and *Springfield, Ohio* (City Hall), Ann Armstrong.

215

Photograph Credits

Page 40—John Schwarz

Page 41—Dan Eisenhart

Page 42—John Ferguson

Page 43—John Newell, Jr.

Pages 44–45—Charles Bayless

Page 46—Courtesy of the Art Commission of the City of New York; bottom, George S. Lewis, FAIA

Page 47—William L. Lebovich

Page 48—Michael Moniz

Page 49—William J. Conklin

Page 50—John Ferguson

Page 51—Anderson Notter Finegold Inc.

Page 52—top right, Kenneth DeMay of Sasaki Associates, Inc.; bottom right, Finlay F. Ferguson, Jr., of William Platt Architect; bottom, Charles Ansell, AIA

Page 53—G. J. Moore, AIA

Page 54—William J. Boney, Jr.

Page 55—Katherine Wetzel

Pages 56–57—Carol Rankin, Anderson Notter Finegold Inc.

Pages 58–59—Utah State Historical Society; page 58, bottom, Robert Hermanson, AIA

Pages 60–61—Michael Karchner

Page 62—Richard Sharpe, FAIA

Page 63—Tessier Associates

Pages 64–65—Jack E. Boucher, HABS

Pages 66–67—Jet Lowe, HABS

Pages 68–69—Jack E. Boucher, HABS; page 68, bottom, Cervin Robinson, HABS

Pages 70–71—Lawrence Tilley, HABS

Page 72—D. Murphy

Page 73—Ning-Kang Lu

Page 74—Stephen Brown, AIA

Page 75—Steve Zane; middle left, Courtesy of Hoboken Library

Page 76—John D. Salvetti, Jr.

Page 77—Hobart Jackson, Jr.

Pages 78–79—John Griebsch

Pages 80–81—Katherine Wetzel

Page 82—Bill Swartz

Page 83—top, Jerome Mejewski; bottom, Courtesy of the City of San Antonio

Page 84—Forest Atkins

Page 85—George Cushing; top left, Longfellow, Alden and Harlow

Page 86—Paul Vecchio

Page 87—Gridley Barrows, AIA

Pages 88–89—Denes A. Saari, Saari and Forrai

Pages 90–91—Walter Smalling, Jr., HABS

Pages 92–93—Robert Pettus

Page 94—Dan Eisenhart

Page 95—Lyle Erlewine

Page 96—Gordon Peery

Page 97—Dallas Swogger

Pages 98–99—Peter Vanderwarker

Page 100—Betsy Swanson

Page 101—Jadel

Pages 102–103—Eric Oxendorf; Jack E. Boucher, HABS

Page 104—Guy Vinson; bottom right, Courtesy of Bancroft Library, University of California, Berkeley

Page 105—Philip Johnson and Leslie Kenyon; top left, Reeves and Bailee, Architects

Pages 106–107—Jack E. Boucher, HABS; top right, Ingle and Almirall

Page 108—LeRoy Langlois

Page 109—Ted Wall

Page 110—Charles Ansell, AIA

Page 111—Louis Barbieri, AIA

Page 112—Brian Gordon

Page 113—Ned Gwinner

Page 114—Gustave Araoz, Jr.

Page 115—Gregory K. Glass

Page 116—Robert Dunn, Arkansas Historic Preservation Program; top right, Arkansas Historic Preservation Program

Page 117—Michael Cipriani

Page 118—Guy Vinson, College of Environmental Design, University of California, Berkeley

Page 119—Robert Faulkner

Page 120—John Giles

Page 121—Robert Van Noy

Pages 122–23—Courtesy of Graphics and Reproduction Center, City of Chicago; page 122, top, Holabird and Roche, Architects, Courtesy of *New York Architect*; page 123, Hedrich-Blessing

Page 124—Thomas Graves, Jr.; bottom right, National Archives

Page 125—Joseph Alicata, Jr.

Page 126—John Barry

Page 127—Jack Porter

Page 128—Guy Vinson, College of Environmental Design, Documents Collection, University of California, Berkeley

Page 129—Bruce Mikle

Page 130—Tibor Gasparik

Page 131—Robert Dunn, Arkansas Historic Preservation Program

Pages 132–33—Gabriel Moulin Studios; page 132, top and bottom, Joseph Baird, Jr.

Page 134—top, Courtesy of Historical Society of Delaware; bottom, John Newell, Jr.

Page 135—Harvey Kelman

Page 136—Richard Boyd

Page 137—Robert Bullock

Pages 138–39—Dennis Marsico

Page 140—Courtesy of Littleton Historical Museum

Page 141—Les Eugene

Page 142—Ronald Fleckal

Page 143—Inge Rose, AIA

Page 144—Julius Shulman

Page 145—Horace Cantrell, AIA, and James Smith, AIA

Pages 146–47—James P. Robinson; page 146, bottom left, and page 147, Dan Forer

Page 148—Wade Lawrence, AIA

Page 149—John Milan

Pages 150–51—Bob Rink

Pages 152–53—Gabriel Benzur

Pages 154–55—Melvyn Schieltz

Pages 156–57—Larry Cohen and Raymond Daniels; page 156, top, and pages 156–57, bottom, Courtesy of John W. Cowper Company, Inc.

Page 158—Donald Strachner, RA, AIA, NCARB

Page 159—Christopher Petrich

Page 160—Shin Koyama

Page 161—Thomas Graves, Jr.

Pages 162–63—Dan Forer; page 163, bottom, Courtesy of Pan American World Airways

Pages 164–65—Paul Kivett

Pages 166–67—Judson Wood

Pages 168–69—Owen Johnson

Page 170—Bill E. Peavler, AIA

Page 171—Luke Dupont

Pages 172–73—Curtis and Mays Studio

Pages 174–75—William L. Lebovich

Pages 176–77—Melissa Allen

Page 178—Gregory Glass

Page 179—J. Paul Ahern, AIA

Pages 180–81—Robert Laws

Pages 182–83—Balthazar Korab

Pages 184–85—Frank Branger

Page 186—Patricia Maley; bottom, John Newell, Jr.

Page 187—Bill Swartz

Page 190—Pasadena, Inge Rose, AIA; Savannah, Ned Gwinner

Page 191—San Francisco, Henry Hope Reed, Jr.; Baltimore, Michael Karchner

Page 192—New York, George S. Lewis, FAIA; Chicopee, Tessier Associates; Springfield, Mass., Joseph Alicata, Jr.

Page 193—Philadelphia, Jack E. Boucher, HABS

Page 194—Yonkers, Michael Cipriani

Page 195—Buffalo, Larry Cohen and Raymond Daniels; Cleveland, Tibor Gasparik

Page 196—North Little Rock, Arkansas Historic Preservation Program; Richmond, Katherine Wetzel

Page 197—Scottsdale, Melissa Allen; Providence, Lawrence Tilley, HABS; Little Rock, Arkansas Historic Preservation Program

Page 198—Minneapolis, Denes A. Saari, Saari and Forrai; The Cabildo, John Ferguson; New York, Courtesy of the Art Commission of the City of New York

Page 199—Richmond, Katherine Wetzel (left), William Edwin Booth, APSA (right)

How to Use the HABS Collection

The photographs, measured drawings and historical information that form the collection of the Historic American Buildings Survey are housed in the Prints and Photographs Division (Architecture, Design and Engineering Collections) of the Library of Congress in Washington, D.C. The division's reading room is open to visitors and researchers. The records, which may be researched using a printed checklist, card catalog and subject card index, are arranged in geographical order: by state, county, city or vicinity and building or project name. Researchers may consult captioned black and white photographs, written histories and photocopies of measured drawings (not all buildings are recorded in all three forms of documentation). Available illustrations and documentation may be retrieved using file numbers based on geographical location; this number also serves as the negative number used to order prints of HABS photographs. Measured drawings carry numbers assigned by HABS as the documentation is created.

In November 1983 a computerized checklist of buildings in the HABS (and Historic American Engineering Record) collection was published as the first effort to list all buildings and sites in both surveys and as the first national catalog to the HABS collections since a 1941 catalog and 1959 supplement. This checklist is intended to serve as a major guide to the collection, both for researchers using the Library of Congress facilities and for those unable to visit Washington. The checklist, following the geographical arrangement, indicates the amount of documentation available for each building or site and the appropriate file numbers.

Several additional aids are available for researching the collection. The Library of Congress can provide a list of publications about the various state and local surveys conducted by HABS and HAER, including all published catalogs, as well as a list of publications that reproduce substantial portions of the collections. Two publications in microfilm and microfiche also may be ordered, one from the Photoduplication Service of the Library of Congress and one from a private publisher, Somerset House. Researchers may request an information packet from the Prints and Photographs Division providing reading and price lists and basic information on the HABS, HAER and division collections.

Copies of all HABS and HAER materials in the Library of Congress may be ordered from the Photoduplication Service. Those making such requests should provide the names and locations of the buildings and type of documentation desired to the Photoduplication Service, Library of Congress, Washington, D.C. 20540. The library will respond with an order form, building identification numbers, type of documentation available and a price quotation. This order form should be returned with proper payment to the Photoduplication Service. The photographs and measured drawings published in this book, as well as supplemental historical information on the buildings pictured, may be ordered in this manner. (Some recent recording projects may not yet have been transmitted to the library.)

Selected Bibliography

Bailyn, Bernard. *New England Merchants in the Seventeenth Century.* New York: Harper and Row, 1955.

Gillette, Howard. "Philadelphia's City Hall: Monument to a New Political Machine." *The Pennsylvania Magazine of History and Biography,* April 1973.

Glaab, Charles, and Brown, A. Theodore. *A History of Urban America.* New York: Macmillan, 1982.

Hines, Thomas S. *Burnham of Chicago: Architect and Planner.* Chicago: University of Chicago Press, 1979.

Hoover, Dwight. *A Teacher's Guide to American Urban History.* Chicago: Quadrangle Books, 1971.

Krout, John A., and Rice, Arnold. *United States Since 1865.* New York: Barnes and Noble, 1977.

Maass, John. "Philadelphia City Hall: Monster or Masterpiece?" *AIA Journal,* February 1965.

Nietzche, Friedrich Wilhem. "Skirmishes in a War with the Age." In *The Twilight of the Idols, or How to Philosophize with a Hammer; The Anti-Christ; Notes to Zarathustra, and Eternal Recurrence,* translated by Anthony M. Ludovici. New York: Macmillan, 1924.

Pevsner, Nikolaus. *A History of Building Types.* Princeton, N.J.: Princeton University Press, 1976.

Placzek, Adolf K., ed. *Macmillan Encyclopedia of Architects.* New York: Macmillan, 1983.

Roth, Leland. *A Concise History of American Architecture.* New York: Harper and Row, 1976.

Schuyler, Montgomery. *American Architecture and Other Writings.* Edited by William H. Jordy and Ralph Coe. Cambridge: Belknap Press, Harvard University Press, 1961.

Smelser, Marshall, and Gundersen, Joan. *American History at a Glance.* 4th ed. New York: Barnes and Noble, 1978.

Warner, Sam Bass. *The Private City: Philadelphia in Three Periods of Its Growth.* Philadelphia: University of Pennsylvania Press, 1968.

Index of City Halls

Index of Architects

Other Books from The Preservation Press

America's Forgotten Architecture
National Trust for Historic Preservation, Tony P. Wrenn, Elizabeth D. Mulloy. The best overview of preservation today, the book surveys in 475 photographs what is worth saving and how to do it. 312 pages, illustrated, bibliography, appendixes. Published by Pantheon Books. $12.95 paperbound.

Fabrics for Historic Buildings
Jane C. Nylander, 3rd edition. A popular guide that gives practical advice on selecting and using reproductions of historic fabrics. A key feature is an illustrated catalog listing 550 reproduction fabrics. Also included are a glossary and list of manufacturers. 160 pages, illustrated, bibliography. $9.95 paperbound.

Wallpapers for Historic Buildings
Richard C. Nylander. This compact handbook shows not only how to select authentic reproductions of historic wallpapers, but also where to buy more than 350 recommended patterns. Arranged according to historical period, this catalog is the first to aid everyone who seeks an appropriate wall covering for an old or historic building. Included are a glossary, reading list and manufacturers' addresses. 128 pages, illustrated, bibliography, appendixes. $9.95 paperbound.

Respectful Rehabilitation: Answers to Your Questions About Old Buildings
Technical Preservation Services, U.S. Department of the Interior. This book answers 150 questions property owners and residents ask about rehabilitating old houses and other historic buildings. The answers are based on the Secretary of the Interior's Standards for Rehabilitation, which are used to determine eligibility for federal rehabilitation tax credits. With the standards and guidelines reprinted in full, an extensive reading list, sources of information. Illustrated with photographs and 100 drawings by David J. Baker. 192 pages, illustrated, bibliography, glossary, appendixes. $9.95 paperbound.

What Style Is It? A Guide to American Architecture
John Poppeliers, S. Allen Chambers, Nancy B. Schwartz, Historic American Buildings Survey. One of the most popular concise guides to American architectural styles, this has just been published in a new format designed for easy identification of buildings at home or on the road. Individual chapters on 22 of the most important styles provide a concise look at the history and appearance of each style. 112 pages, illustrated, glossary, bibliography. $6.95 paperbound.

To order Preservation Press books, send total of book prices (less 10 percent discount for National Trust members), plus $2.50 postage and handling, to: Preservation Bookshop, 1600 H Street, N.W., Washington, D.C. 20006. Residents of California, the District of Columbia, Massachusetts, New York and South Carolina please add applicable sales tax.